# Becoming a
# CULINARY
# ARTS
# PROFESSIONAL

# Becoming a

# CULINARY ARTS PROFESSIONAL

LearningExpress®

New York

Copyright © 2010 Learning Express, LLC.

All rights reserved under International and Pan American Copyright Conventions.
Published in the United States by LearningExpress, LLC, New York.

Library of Congress Cataloging-in-Publication Data:
Becoming a culinary arts professional : find your rewarding career in the world of food.
   p.  cm.
  ISBN-13 978-1-57685-739-7
  1.  Food service—Vocational guidance.    I.  LearningExpress (Organization)
  TX911.3.V62B45   2010
  647.95023—dc22

                                        2010006918

Printed in the United States of America

9  8  7  6  5  4  3  2  1

ISBN-13 978-1-57685-739-7

For more information or to place an order, contact LearningExpress® at:
  2 Rector Street
  26th Floor        •
  New York, NY 10006

Or visit us at:
  www.learnatest.com

Direct any questions or comments to:
  customerservice@learningexpressllc.com

# Contents

# Introduction

*Cooking is one of the oldest arts and one which has rendered us the most important service in civic life.*

—Jean Anthelme Brillat-Savarin

**DO YOU** want the opportunity to work with food, earn a good living, and meet lots of interesting people? If so, a career in the culinary arts may be just what you are looking for. Whether you are choosing your first career or are considering a career change, this book was designed for you. It contains all the information you will need to get started in this exciting field.

The culinary arts field is one of the fastest growing in the country. According to the National Restaurant Association, the restaurant industry employs an estimated 13 million people, or 9% of the U.S. workforce, and is expected to add 1.8 million jobs over the next ten years. By 2019, restaurant employment is forecast to reach 14.8 million people. However, restaurant work is only one of the many areas where culinary professionals find great jobs. Catering, hotels, food retail, institutional food service, personal and private chefs, media food styling and photography, recipe testing and developing, cooking instruction, and the host of career areas related to culinary products make the restaurant association's outlook even more optimistic.

This book will provide you with an overview of this vast field and the many exciting opportunities for culinary professionals. It also navigates the wide range of routes to training and certification. If you are just finishing high school and choosing a vocation, you will find reasons you might want to choose a culinary profession and help discern exactly which niche best suits you. If you are changing careers, either by choice or of necessity, you will learn how advantageous it can be to transfer the skills and experience you have already accumulated from your previous profession and jump-start a new food-related occupation. If you are already working in a kitchen, but have no degree or certification, you will find help here for mapping out a satisfying, upwardly mobile career path through which you can earn a solid livelihood.

> *I was 32 when I started cooking. Up to then I just ate.*
>
> —Julia Child

If there is one overarching message of this book, it is that there are many culinary professions, dynamic options for training, and countless ways to succeed. You may combine culinary arts with almost any other skill or interest. You can choose full-time, part-time, even online training. (Many study the food arts via evening or weekend programs while supporting themselves and their families through full-time work! The older student is becoming more common—and welcome—in cooking schools.) You could pursue a prestigious degree at a well-known culinary institute, or just start with a basic food handling certificate, which generally requires no on-site classes.

Perhaps no line of business has such a broad range of entry points, and yet such a concise body of core skills and necessary information, as the culinary arts industry. The first three chapters of this book help you explore these options and detail how to gain the proper training to succeed. Although much culinary skill and information are tested hands-on, Chapter 4 consists of two practice tests that include the key questions you are most likely to encounter on a written culinary exam. Each of the two tests is divided into five culinary skill sets. A third practice test is available on the LearningExpress website. Visit www.learnatest.com/practice to access this test.

This book will introduce you to everything you need to know about cooking and the food world. Whether you have had a previous career or you are just starting out, may it help guide you to true success: a career that allows you to make the most of your unique passions, talents, desires, and skills. Being able to do so is the secret ingredient to creating a great first or second career.

# Becoming a
# CULINARY
# ARTS
# PROFESSIONAL

# CHAPTER one

## WHY THE CULINARY WORLD?

**WHEREVER WE** turn, we run into images of food or food personalities. In contrast to 20 or certainly 30 years ago, when there were relatively few television programs devoted exclusively to food, we now have an entire network devoted to food-related programming. Food-related programs also appear both on network and on cable stations. Unlike in the past, in the media world of today the focus of food programs is on food as entertainment. Food programming is often a type of reality show, with contestants vying to win over their chef competitors. We cheer for the winners and feel sorry for the losers—and look forward to tuning in again next week.

Years ago, television programs focused on instructional programming. Viewers were taught and shown, in detail, how to bone a chicken, reduce a sauce, or blend ingredients to make the lightest of cakes. In our contemporary society—with its emphasis on fast food, meals in 20 minutes, takeout meals, and abundant prepared-food options—we turn to food-related media for entertainment rather than instruction. However one feels about the return of the instructional cooking show, the fact is that more people than ever before are being exposed to the world of food. And that has resulted in more people considering a culinary arts career than ever before.

Health is another growing area of concern, and this, too, is reflected in TV programming. Obesity, diabetes, and other illnesses than can be managed through diet are leading many to explore careers where they learn about and then practice the preparation of healthy food.

## ATTRACTIONS OF THE FOOD WORLD

What makes a recent high school or college graduate, or even a career changer at any age, want to enter this clearly fast-paced, incredibly competitive world? Partly it is because we are fascinated by the personalities of celebrity chefs, the allure of the culinary lifestyle, the glamour of top restaurants, the healing of spas, and the drama that surrounds it all.

Anyone who is curious about entering the culinary world must answer two key questions: Why do I think this is a career for me? and How do I get there?

It is important to realize that the TV programming we see more and more is just that—programming. It is designed to entertain audiences, not to educate them to the realities of the industry. These shows, as well as articles, profiles, and books on the subject, often show only one side of this complex field.

The fact is that few chefs make it to the level of a media celebrity with their own chain of restaurants, product line, and nationally syndicated television show. Often we are led to think that the path to the top is far quicker than it is in reality, because we are spared from seeing the bumps and jolts along the way.

It is, in fact, possible to complete a culinary education in a relatively short time, even a few months for full-time diploma programs. In the book *The Apprentice*, one of the truly great autobiographies from a master chef, Jacques Pépin relates his own early years training in the kitchen in France.

It was the tradition then to spend several years working at prep functions in the kitchen before ever being allowed to so much as stand at a stove. Things have certainly changed.

While glamour and the quest for celebrity can be powerful motivators, look elsewhere for motivators that can allow you to stay with the long hours and competition that are realities in the field.

Indeed there can be glamorous moments. What young chef would not want to be cooking for a star-studded banquet? And while he or she may be greeted and thanked by the rich and famous, that glamour can instantly fade in the face of the organizational details of pulling together such an event.

## WHAT ATTRACTS *YOU* TO THE CULINARY ARTS?

For many people, the decision to enter the culinary arts stems directly from their love of food. Whether that love of food was created from a happy childhood filled with memories of a warm kitchen surrounded by different delicious smells, or from a trip abroad where they experienced an incredible dish, or from a love of reading cookbooks and experimenting in their own kitchen, it is a passion that pulls many people into this field. Of course, there are also very practical reasons to enter the field. Job security, the opportunity for advancement, or the desire not to work in a 9-to-5 office setting may influence one's decision.

When you reflect on what attracts you to the food world, aside from a love and passion for food, it is crucial to consider in what kind of environment you are most comfortable working. Are you energized by working around other people? Do you thrive on controlled chaos and the adrenalin rush? Do you prefer to work by yourself undisturbed? Even in the food world, would you prefer a desk job? Or do you like to be out and about and not restricted to an office environment? These are all crucial questions to ask yourself.

One of the great attractions for students coming into the culinary profession is its versatility. Jobs are available in virtually any place in the country, and around the world, at a variety of levels. And even in harder economic times, there is generally a need for workers with cooking skills, because people do not stop eating out but instead will go to less expensive eateries or pick up prepared items from the grocery gourmet section—still prepared by a culinary arts professional.

The restaurant world is the most visible and consequently the target of most students interested in pursuing the path of the culinary professional. The reality of that work, at least for the newly initiated, is absolutely low pay, long—often very long—hours, the need for physical stamina, and an established hierarchy of personalities and jobs to work through and negotiate.

## CULINARY SELF-QUESTIONNAIRE

Now that you know what attracts you to a career in the culinary arts, you are probably starting to get excited about your future career. A critical next step is to ask yourself, *Do I have what it takes to make it in this competitive industry?* Success generally requires the ability to work as a part of a team, discipline, personal cleanliness, organizational skills, physical stamina, and a keen sense of taste and smell. Take a few moments to consider the following questions to help you evaluate whether a career in the world of food is a good match for your skills and interests.

*Do I want to actually prepare food or would I prefer to be around food?*

_____

*What are my images of the food world and in what type of culinary position do I see myself?*

_____

_____

_____

_____

Answer true or false to the following statements:

| *True* | *False* | |
|--------|---------|---|
| ❑ | ❑ | I can tolerate very long hours. |
| ❑ | ❑ | I am happy to work closely with other people. |
| ❑ | ❑ | I enjoy the adrenalin rush of constant demands. |
| ❑ | ❑ | I have physical stamina, can lift heavy boxes, and can stand on my feet for hours. |
| ❑ | ❑ | I am comfortable working within an established hierarchy of personalities. |
| ❑ | ❑ | I like to be out and about. |
| ❑ | ❑ | I possess basic math skills. |
| ❑ | ❑ | I am detail oriented. |
| ❑ | ❑ | I am fine working evenings and weekends when most people are off from work. |
| ❑ | ❑ | I am a good problem solver. |
| ❑ | ❑ | I love and have a passion for food. |
| ❑ | ❑ | I thrive on controlled chaos. |
| ❑ | ❑ | I am comfortable working in a stressful environment. |
| ❑ | ❑ | I enjoy working with the public and have strong customer service skills. |
| ❑ | ❑ | I am willing to move any place in the country. |

If you answered *true* to the majority of these questions, you may have strong potential in the culinary arts. If you answered *true* to all of them, it may be time for you to talk to a career counselor or admissions advisor and investigate starting an internship or enrolling in culinary classes.

Only you can make the final decision to enter the culinary field. But you do not have to reach that decision alone. Besides seeking professional career advice, talk to people in the field. Ask them about their experiences and their impressions of the advantages and disadvantages of their jobs. This type of networking will serve you well as you enter the field, as well as throughout your career.

## THE CULINARY MARKETPLACE TODAY

The restaurant industry is the nation's second largest private-sector employer. In 2009, growth in the industry again outpaced growth in the overall economy for the ninth consecutive year. Future growth looks consistently optimistic as the industry is projected to add more than a million new jobs over the next ten years.

Salaries for culinary professionals vary greatly depending on the type and size of the establishment. Some restaurants provide employees with free uniforms and free meals, but federal law permits employers to deduct from their employees' wages the cost of any meals or lodging provided, and some will do so. Chefs, cooks, and other kitchen workers who work full time may receive benefits such as vacation days, sick days, health insurance, and retirement savings plans, but part-time workers generally do not. Benefits are more likely to be available in large, well-established hotels, institutions, or franchise restaurants. Many small independent restaurants cannot afford to offer them.

As in any other industry, the pay rate is proportionate to the number of jobs available. The Bureau of Labor Statistics reports that in 2009, the mean hourly wage for foodservice industry jobs was $10 for chefs and cooks and less for assistants—only half of the national mean hourly wage. Jobs in the food and beverage industry are plentiful but it will take work and training and time to overcome the reality of a low earnings. The following table provides current salary guidelines for culinary professionals.

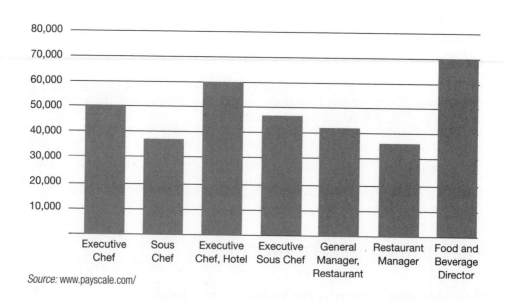

Source: www.payscale.com/

The average salaries shown in the table are indeed lower than in many other industries, which can be a challenge for many people. Keep in mind, however, that experienced line cooks, sous and executive chefs, and restaurant managers who work in upscale restaurants, large hotels, or restaurant chains can make significantly more than the average salaries listed earlier.

Other good news is that projections for growth rates for the culinary industry over the next years are strong. Jobs with the fastest growth rates are expected to be management positions, chefs, head cooks, and waitstaff. Furthermore, the industry shows a great deal of internal movement as part-time workers gain more experience and compete for full-time work. Positions at the entry level are consistently opening up.

## Statistics and Trends

The marketplace for workers in the food and beverage industry unquestionably represents a cornerstone in the U.S. economy. The 2009 National Restaurant Association reports annual sales of $566 billion in nearly 1 million restaurant and foodservice outlets nationwide. Given the accessibility and value proposition of many restaurant outlets in the country, the report found nearly half of all consumers' food budget was spent in restaurants. Surprisingly, the results varied little by region; those in small towns might choose a diner rather than a restaurant, but across the nation, everyone eats out.

In addition, the survey recognize 13 million employees in the industry to represent a substantial 9% of the U.S. workforce. Despite the recent economic downturn, the industry is projected to show increases in sales in 2010 and beyond and represents 4% of all U.S. gross domestic product. In short, the culinary industry is projected to remain stable.

Finally, two other factors figure in this profile of the market today. In general, the restaurant world is a young population: current surveys indicate that 37% of workers are below the age of 24. In addition, the bulk of the work is part-time, a higher percentage than in other U.S. industries.

## Where the Jobs Are

Food jobs are available just about everywhere. However, you should take certain geographical factors and trends into consideration when deciding where to pursue work. During the next ten years, Texas, Nevada, Colorado, New Mexico, and Arizona are expected to show the strongest percentages of growth in this industry. Along with Florida, which has already shown consistently strong growth, Texas and Nevada are expected to show the fastest increases in job growth, faster by nearly 25% than other top states. This growth represents opportunities at all levels, from food preparation to servers to chefs to executives.

The top trends in restaurant food both for full-service eateries and for fast-service operators focus on value and healthier food choices and eating options. More new restaurants and consumer products boasting healthy, organic, or vitamin-enhanced or low-fat food options are becoming available all the time. An establishment's ability to incorporate locally grown produce and to utilize green practices is becoming increasingly important to consumers and influences where they shop for food and where they choose to eat. Even quick-service restaurants and chains are exploring how to incorporate locally grown ingredients into their menus. Plus, for the first time healthy menu options for children are appearing as a growing trend in fast-food retail.

With higher grocery store prices and the continued crunch for leisure time, many consumers rank the value that a restaurant can provide (in terms of price, quality, healthfulness, and so on) as a top motivator in eating out regularly.

## FACTORS TO CONSIDER IN CHOOSING A CULINARY CAREER

The range of workers entering the culinary world has never been more diverse and the universe of culinary opportunities is more visible than ever because of the tremendous media exposure available today. These circumstances entice workers of all ages and levels of training into this exciting industry.

Culinary schools and programs are now seeing a wider diversity in such factors as age, geographic origin, and level of world experience than ever before. The profile of a new culinary student is no longer only the post–high school or –college student looking for a vocation. Certainly that profile still exists, but the face of today's culinary student can look quite different. It is not uncommon to see culinary arts students in their late 20s or early 30s who have had some success in the workforce, but who for whatever reason have decided their original careers were not for them and are making a career change.

More interesting is the emerging group of workers age 40 and over who are entering the profession. This group includes retired workers who want to continue to work as well as the large population who, in recent years, have been downsized in their careers and need to retrain and look elsewhere for work. The tremendous new cultural diversity of students contributes to the quality of culinary programs today. This is a new workforce, and the good news in the culinary world is that there are opportunities to join at any age and without regard to race, gender, or national heritage, or whether one has had any prior culinary training.

With a job market changing and evolving at such a high rate, one key skill that is essential to ensure industry success is flexibility. It is clearly the employee who is able to adapt his or her skill set to new opportunities and possibilities who will have the advantage over a worker with a narrower focus. In fact, the current marketplace can be particularly beneficial for career changers who are able to bring not only their knowledge of food but also an entire skill set from previous work experience.

Up to this point, we have focused on some of the realities and opportunities of working in the restaurant world. Many aspiring culinary professionals aim straight for the line in a restaurant kitchen, but the expanding food world now offers hundreds more opportunities. So, flexibility is also a factor when you consider what type of path you want to take in your culinary career. While it may make sense for you to start in a restaurant, there may be another equally viable path for you to take to achieve your ultimate career goal. The key is to identify your individual culinary interests and skill sets and match them to the right job for you.

If, for example, you have decided you *do* want to be a chef, your happiness may depend largely on *where* you decide to be a chef. Aside from traditional restaurants, there are opportunities for chefs in private homes, on yachts, with airline companies, in corporate dining rooms, in hospitals, in schools, in bed-and-breakfasts, with catering companies, in television studios, in bakeries, and so on. Even before you start your culinary training, it is important to think about the environment in which you are most comfortable working. This self-assessment will help you to be focused from the beginning and get the most out of your education.

Alternatively, if you have decided you want to prepare food but do not like the pace of the restaurant world, perhaps the world of specialty food retail is a good fit for you. This area would give you an opportunity to work with the public and allow you to share your passion for food with customers without the responsibilities of cooking, plating, and serving. This is a career path where it is easy to develop a specialty. Why not become a specialty cheese importer? or an artisanal bread baker? or a gourmet shop owner?

The world of food media is another world of opportunity. If you prefer not to handle food directly, but have an interest and fascination, you might write about food for television production companies, magazines, book publishers, or freelance as a restaurant reviewer, a publicist, an archivist, a researcher, an editor, a recipe developer, or even a blogger.

Another area not to overlook, particularly if you come from a first career in the business world, is the area of management and finance. All good food businesses need strategists, analysts, accountants, and managers. Working in your new career in an area in which you have had some previous expertise can be exciting and fulfilling.

This is a just a brief introduction to the myriad jobs available in the culinary world. We will investigate the range of culinary jobs in more detail in Chapter 2.

## A CAREER-CHANGER/CULINARY PROFESSIONAL'S STORY

I always loved good food. I grew up in a family where dinner was lovingly cooked every night by my mother. I came home to simmering soups and freshly made casseroles for supper. The meals I enjoyed when I visited my friends, more often than not, consisted of home-cooked roasts, soups, stews and, of course, a full cookie jar and the occasional cake or pan of brownies. For me, the flavors and smells of good cooking represented bringing people together and enjoying life.

Years later when I was out on my own for the first time, confronted with any empty kitchen, there was no roast in the oven, nor any cookies in the jar. Living on a modest salary, I had to choose between spending money I did not have by eating out or make the effort to learn to cook. My initial attempts were feeble at best and usually included several phone calls to my mother in an attempt to have her explain why the banana bread was soggy or why the roast chicken was somehow still raw inside. I learned a lot in these early years. Memories of those days sustained me because I knew that someday I would make a serious attempt to understand food and make cooking a part of my life.

Years later, when my career in marketing had grown enough that I had the luxury of time to cook, I branched out from the four dishes (three of them included pasta) that I could make with some certainty they would be edible to me and my friends. I started to discover and read cookbooks and cooking magazines and try my hand at more adventurous meals. I loved having friends over and showing them the hospitality that a good meal expresses.

Then I was fortunate enough to work on some culinary related projects in my corporate life that I enjoyed tremendously. I decided to take a recreational cooking class to better understand culinary terminology and methods and to more effectively handle those projects. Intrigued, I started taking class after class, gaining new knowledge and having fun. I was learning, step by step, how to cook.

When downsizings and layoffs hit the company where I worked, as they have for so many businesses, I was faced with a decision: try to find a job in another company doing what I had always done, or try something new. I had spent nearly 20 years in one industry. Was it time to do what I really *loved*?

After talking with a number of friends and colleagues, I decided it was indeed time to focus on something new and entirely different. I had yet to connect what I loved doing and combine it with my own innate, as well as learned, skills. I was no longer going to work in the traditional marketing roles I had known, but was determined to find a way not to waste all those years and take some of that experience into this new world of food.

Since I was coming into culinary arts as a mid-life career changer, I felt that getting an actual culinary diploma would be the best route for me. I was in my mid-forties and did not have the years of apprenticeship and working my way up in the food world that experienced culinary professionals typically had at my age. I needed new training that was fast, comprehensive, reliable and that could put me on my new road as quickly as possible.

# Becoming a CULINARY ARTS PROFESSIONAL

My experience once in culinary school was a combination of hard work, great camaraderie, and deep pride and accomplishment. I was, by far, the oldest in the class and having had a nearly 20-year corporate career behind me, was able to bring a sense of organization and management to my team and the execution of our daily dishes. I also enjoyed learning from my younger classmates, who brought their fresh perspectives to my views about food.

As I neared the end of my studies, the issue of what I was going to do occupied my mind daily. I have always loved the experience of dining in a good restaurant, yet the excitement and the adrenalin of a restaurant kitchen, I knew, was not going to be the route for me. Working in a professional kitchen (whether in a high-speed, high-profile metropolitan restaurant or a small neighborhood diner or bakery) takes stamina, strength, and long hours that just weren't for me. I had paid my dues in my early career years and wanted a different pace now. The world of working the line, delivering 150 covers (orders of food) each night wasn't going to be for me.

Given my previous career, media was a logical place for me to look. The Career Placement office at my culinary school sent me to several volunteer jobs to get a sense of what might be available and gain a bit of experience combining my old field with my new one. I did some editing of articles about food and felt like the world's oldest intern at a TV production company for a cooking program. These experiences were a good transfer of the skills I had mastered in the corporate world, but they didn't allow me to touch food, much less be involved with cooking it. (An aside about being an older intern is that we are more and more common, accepted, and valued. Once I checked my ego, it was great to be in a situation where not only could I get on-the-job experience in my new career, but also contribute way more than the host organization expected!)

My greatest insight as to what my new career would be about was still to come. One day, I was asked to go to a newly opened education center that was developing courses for recreational students in food and wine. I was being asked to assist or *stage* for the chef. I was excited by this opportunity since it involved a class, working with students and getting them excited to cook. Working with the chef in the class, answering students' questions, listening to the conversations, helped me move my new career forward significantly.

Marketing at its essence is listening and communicating. Whether with a large audience or a small one, marketers are trying to engage consumers with what's exciting, new, and relevant about the products they sell. Teaching, as I reflected on it that particular day, was exactly the same thing. Good teachers need to *sell* their content and make it relevant, exciting, curious, and meaningful for their students. They also need that marketing instinct for connecting with people. In that moment, it all came together for me. I knew where and how my key skill set would and could be useful and desirable in my new world of food—as a culinary educator. I would be able to touch food, teach food, and with my highly trained ability to speak and present in front of the public, I would most likely be able to hold a class's interest and have fun doing so.

About a month after I graduated from culinary school, I taught my first class on the fundamentals of cooking in front of twelve excited and eager students, all ready to discover the world of cooking for themselves. I was right where I belonged. In building a culinary career, I have taken advantage of the writing, editing, and management skills that I honed in my corporate years, but the bulk of my work is as a chef-instructor, and that is where I am most fulfilled.

—Carl Raymond
New York City

## Culinary Skill Set

When asked, *What do you think will make you a successful culinary arts professional?* most people will answer, *Well, I love food.* That is a great answer, because a love of food is certainly the fuel that can keep you going in an often tough career path. However, that love of food most often means a love of *eating* food. As a culinary professional you will certainly taste and have the chance to enjoy your fair share of wonderful, creative dishes, whatever your chosen culinary path, but what will truly sustain you in the industry is your unique skill set and talents.

The key to standing out from the rest is your ability to explain your skill set to an employer, indicating how you can apply it in the job you are applying for. Your skill set is your magic toolbox; it will be as essential to your career success as your new kit of shiny, sharp knives. Whether you are a student considering entering the culinary world right out of high school or an adult creating a whole new career, make sure you understand what marketable skills you already have and what new skills you need to acquire.

An ideal skill set that will serve you well in the culinary arts, regardless of age or life experience, includes the following:

teamwork
leadership

flexibility
curiosity
stamina
basic math skills

Let us see how this skill set applies to various possibilities in the culinary world.

Whether you work in a major corporation or at the tiniest bakery, a sense of **teamwork** is essential. In the culinary world, particularly in the areas of food preparation, you will rarely hold all the responsibility yourself. For example, in a commercial kitchen, you may be responsible for executing several dishes as part of your responsibilities, but you will find yourself dependent on your coworkers for additional components of those meals or other dishes to make up the entire menu being served. If you lack the proper teamwork to have the meal timed correctly, it will not matter that you have prepared the perfect filet mignon, because you will not have the roasted potatoes to serve with it. Teamwork involves excellent, clear communication, trust, and organization.

**Leadership** involves taking a sense of responsibility in order to get a job accomplished. In the culinary world, this can mean taking the initiative on a task that you know needs to be done, without waiting to be asked. Teamwork and leadership are complementary skills. It is important that you display leadership in how you complete your tasks, even as you support your team to the finish line. A solid work ethic, the ability to prioritize, and, again, good communication are all traits of a good leader. Imagine you are in the middle of your shift (what most chefs refer to as *service*), at the height of the dinner rush, and your colleague is *deep in the weeds* (an expression chefs use to refer to being overwhelmed with orders). Would you not jump in and do what you could to help, while maintaining your own responsibilities?

**Flexibility** is perhaps the most important skill for a culinary arts professional. It means being able to roll with the punches but still get the job done. What if a key employee calls in sick the day of an important banquet? What if the special ingredient you ordered weeks before suddenly is not available when you need it? What if one of your ovens stops functioning in the middle of service? You must be able to think clearly and act immediately in a variety of challenging situations and complete the job as if you had all your anticipated tools and team in place. In the culinary world—as is most of life—you will always run into the unexpected, but the unexpected is rarely an acceptable excuse for failure. Flexibility is essential, not only in reactions but also in planning. Yes, it is even a good idea to anticipate what *might* happen and to come up with an alternative plan in your head, just in case.

A **curious palate** is akin to a love of eating good food, and will certainly help sustain you in a culinary career. Truly to succeed, and to have the widest variety of job possibilities open to you, it is important to have an ongoing curiosity about food and be willing to continue to educate yourself by attending classes. What is the science behind emulsion sauces? Will I get the same result whether I use a Meyer lemon or a regular lemon? Which cuts of meat taste best when prepared by which cooking methods? Thousands of questions exist, and a truly successful culinary professional will seek as many of the answers as possible. We cook today with the widest variety of ingredients, and questions about new ingredients—Where did they come from? How are they grown? How do they affect taste?—occupy the mind of the curious culinary artist. One of the most exciting things about working in the culinary world is having just this kind of conversations with your colleagues, who are all wondering and experimenting along with you. You will never know all there is to know about food, and no individual in the industry does. A good chef is always learning and sharing information; this prevents the industry from ever becoming static.

One of the essential—and most overlooked—skills is **stamina**. If your ultimate niche is in one of the hands-on jobs in the culinary world, you will find you need a great deal of stamina. The hours are long; the conditions are hot and can be uncomfortable. Your best friend is a good pair of sturdy, comfortable shoes, because you will work standing up for hours on end. The culinary world is not one in which you sit down very often.

> *I remember one freelance job I was doing for a media company, testing and developing recipes. When I walked out the door after an eight-hour shift and sat down on the bus to come home, I realized the last time I had been sitting that day was on that very same bus coming to work that morning.*
>
> —A culinary professional

The hours can be long. Even after a shift has officially ended, there always seems to be more work to do: refrigerators to clean, floors to mop, prep to be done for the next day, shelves to reorganize for better efficiency, and on and on. The bulk of hands-on jobs involves lifting, bending, stretching, and often slicing, dicing, or chopping on a counter of less-than-ideal height. Space is often tight, and those ovens can get hot. Indeed, a professional kitchen working at full tilt brings a great sense of drama and the rush of adrenalin to its cooks who have the stamina to handle the physical realities.

### Insider's Advice

*When I was working from 8 to 12 hours a day as a chef, I started making time to go to the health club to get in better physical shape to handle the long days. It takes a lot out of you, so no matter how busy you are, you still have to take time out for yourself.*

—Chef Cannataro

You may be surprised to find that having **basic math skills** can play a key role in your culinary career. While math is especially important in the pastry and baking specializations, basic math is used by all culinary professionals, including cooks and chefs. For example, you may need to halve a recipe to make a smaller portion of a particular dish, or you may need to expand the recipe to serve 60 people instead of 10. Or perhaps you will need to convert a recipe from a country that uses the metric system. All in all, you will need to pay attention to detail and be comfortable with basic math to ensure that your measurements, and your dishes, come out as planned.

## ARE YOU SUITED TO THE CULINARY PROFESSION?

Now that you know what some key skills could be, take some time to think back on your own experiences and see where you have been. No matter whether you have never had a professional job or whether you have a 30-year career behind you, you can learn and develop skills at any stage in your life.

Take a few minutes (you may want to grab a pencil and some paper) to think about the following questions. As you will see, each set of questions in this self-assessment relates directly to the skill sets just discussed. You need not answer every single question right away. This exercise is designed to get you to start thinking about your unique experience and how you can use it to find a niche in the culinary world.

1. Think back to a time when you were part of a team. Perhaps you were a member of a sports team or participated in a task force in a corporate setting. Were you the designated leader? What did you like most about the experience? What did you like least? Did you like the experience of leading or did you prefer to be led by someone else? If the team worked well together, why do think that was? If it did not, what do you think happened?

2. Do you naturally volunteer to take charge if you are in a situation when a leader is asked for? Is it easier for you to formulate strategic ideas or do you prefer to execute someone else's requests?

3. How comfortable do you think you are with change? Do you easily adapt to new work environments and new colleagues? Think back to an instance where you might have been given a new work assignment by your supervisor or had a challenging new research assignment to do in school. Did the challenge of the unknown excite you or frustrate you? How did you handle it in the end, and what happened? Did you find that the experience fueled your creativity or shut you down?

4. Imagine a world where you would not have to work to earn money at all. How would you spend your time? If you say, *I'd want to work with food!* That's great. But think about your ideal job: would you travel? stay and build your own business? open a cooking school in Europe? Think about your passions, hobbies, and interests. For example, if you love food and children, would you be happy teaching cooking skills to children? The idea here is to find out what drives you most, because that is the key to finding out what will sustain you on the path to completing your culinary education and knowing where to look for your first job.

5. How physically active are you in your daily life? Do you exercise regularly? Are your knees and back strong? Do you maintain a gym membership? Think about your own physical shape.

As you worked through the self-assessment, what examples came to mind? List several key experiences you have had in your life that you can use as examples to demonstrate your skills. Did you find out that you are less comfortable leading than being given specific directions by someone else? Did you remember a time when you were captain of a sports team or head of a school club? Do you think you were an effective leader? Or perhaps if you come from a longer previous working career, was there a particular project that you managed that challenged your sense of flexibility and how you react to change? Think again, and make a list of three experiences that displayed your talents especially well.

1. _____

2. _____

3. _____

Most people entering a culinary career do, in fact, imagine themselves working in a commercial restaurant, whether small or large, and that that is where most of the jobs in the culinary industry do exist. Even if you are not the executive chef or even the chef de cuisine, there are dozens of supporting jobs that are essential to keep the operation running smoothly.

One of the most exciting things about the current state of the culinary world, however, is that there is an enormous range of other jobs that do not require exactly the same skill sets as working in a restaurant. You can still be as involved—hands on or not—with food preparation. Some of these other jobs can take even better advantage of the skill set you have already been developing in your life.

In the following chapter, we will examine these areas in more detail and help you find your niche in the industry. Pack your knives; you are on your way!

# CHAPTER two

## CULINARY OPPORTUNITIES: FINDING YOUR NICHE

**IN THIS** chapter, we will take a closer look at several options for specific career paths in the culinary world. We will take an inside look at the restaurant world and its structure, the business of catering, opportunities in the hospitality industry, the fast-growing retail culinary field, institutional food service, working as a personal chef, styling and photographing food, testing and developing recipes, and selling and marketing culinary products, so you can begin to imagine what career may work best for you.

## THE WORLD OF RESTAURANTS

Restaurants come in all shapes and sizes, but as you start to think about the best work environment for you, it helps to know something about the structure of a classic formal restaurant. While some high-end restaurants do use this structure, it is more common to find variations with many fewer positions (or *stations*) than you would find in the classic organization.

A restaurant kitchen depends on hierarchy, responsibility, and teamwork. Sounds a bit like the military, right? Not surprisingly, then, the structure of the modern professional kitchen was developed by the French chef Georges Auguste Escoffier, who had been a military officer, serving as chef de cuisine. Aside from his contributions to the preparation of classic French cuisine, he structured his staff at London's Savoy Hotel in the late 19th century on the idea of the *kitchen brigade*. Even today, the names of the rankings in the kitchen are given in French, following Escoffier's model.

### Executive Chef, or Chef de Cuisine

The culinary hierarchy begins with its general, the executive chef (sometimes called the chef de cuisine). This title is reserved for chefs who have achieved an impressive place in their career based on significant education, professional experience, and skill. An executive chef may or may not handle some of the actual cooking but is often responsible for plating and making sure the quality is maintained in each dish that leaves for the dining room. The executive chef is responsible for establishing the menu and creating new dishes. Finally, the executive chef hires and fires staff, manages productivity, and ensures the overall quality of the food.

### Sous Chef

Directly subordinate to the executive chef is the sous chef. (*Sous* literally means *under* in French.) The sous (pronounced *soo*) chef may be in charge when the executive chef is not present. Depending on the size and type of the restaurant, there may be more than one sous chef. Occasionally, the sous chef is responsible for the final plating and presentation but most often coordinates the cooking, or *firing*, of individual dishes in the kitchen. The sous chef constantly checks on the orders as they come in and makes sure each diner's meal is coordinated to be ready to go out to the dining room. A sous chef may also train new hires, inspect the work of other cooks, and order supplies. This job is often regarded as the last step before becoming a full chef.

### Insider's Advice

*The world of a restaurant kitchen is exciting, daunting, theatrical, and extremely well organized if it's going to work. A line cook needs to develop the ability to handle several dishes at once, all in different stages of preparation, and guarantee that they will be executed identically and to the customer's satisfaction night after night.*

—A culinary professional

## Chef de Partie

In many professional kitchens, the kitchen staff is referred to as a *brigade*, a French term for kitchen workers. Since every professional kitchen is different, the number of people making up the brigade in each kitchen will vary. A small kitchen may employ only an executive and a sous chef, while a large kitchen may include 20 or more chefs de partie, or chefs who specialize in one area, or station. Each station in the kitchen is responsible for a different cooking preparation, and each is headed by a chef de partie, who reports directly to the sous chef. The traditional stations include *saucier* (sauces), *poissonier* (fish), *grillardin* (grilled foods), *rotissier* (roasted foods), *fritteurier* (fried foods), *patissieur* (pastry and desserts), and *garde manger* (cold foods, appetizers, and salads).

## Tournant, or *Roundsman*

In larger restaurants, there is a tournant, or *roundsman* (also called a *swing cook*) who is trained to work at any of the stations and can help out at whichever station needs help during the course of a busy shift, or take over if one of the chefs de partie is unavailable. This position can be particularly beneficial because it allows one to become proficient at every station in a particular restaurant.

## Demi Chef and Commis

Subordinate to the chefs de partie are the assistants (*demi chefs*) and the apprentices (*commis*). For recent graduates, an entry-level role would usually be that of demi chef, and interns would usually find themselves working as commis. These assistants prepare food by cutting, measuring, cleaning, peeling, or grinding. They may also stir and strain soups and sauces. The assistant has an important role in a food establishment, because all of these tasks help to save the more experienced chef time and effort. In many kitchens, one can land a position as an assistant without any previous experience; highly selective upscale restaurants, on the other hand, will expect some academic or hands-on training. Assistants usually start at minimum wage.

### Insider's Advice

*My advice to people who are considering a culinary arts career is to go to work in a restaurant—find a job as an assistant cook in a professional kitchen. In a small restaurant kitchen, you may be able to work side by side with the chef. However, in a large hotel kitchen, you may be working among 70 or 80 people and never even meet the head chef. Look at several different eating establishments and ask to work a day in each of their kitchens to get a feel for the different types of working environments. When you land your first job, ask lots of questions, listen closely to the answers, work hard, volunteer for extracurricular activities, and continue to read everything you can get your hands on— cookbooks, magazines, professional books, cooking/food blogs, etc.*

—Ann Cooper, executive chef and 25-year industry veteran

In establishments other than fine-dining restaurants, you may find chefs occupying more than one of these roles, or slight variations in the organization. In general, however, most serious restaurants have adapted some form of this structure, so it is very useful to have at least a basic understanding of restaurant kitchen organization. Large commercial restaurant chains and fast-food establishments have their own systems based on corporate decisions about efficiency, cleanliness, and economy of scale, yet are still based on a hierarchy model.

## FROM YOUR KITCHEN TO A RESTAURANT KITCHEN: WHAT IS THE DIFFERENCE?

People often wonder what differentiates a restaurant cook from a home cook. Could an experienced home cook not turn out a classic sole meunière as well as a chef in a restaurant? Or have you ever been to a well-respected restaurant when someone at your table commented that they thought they could make the same dish at home?

It is true that culinary skill can be developed so that the results of a restaurant chef can be reproduced at home with the right kitchen, the right experience, and the right equipment. What truly distinguishes restaurant chefs is the environment in which they cook and the unique set of skills they gain as a result of the usual fast pace of the restaurant world. A restaurant chef, having executed the same five dishes (or even single dish) many times a night, seven nights a week, will know almost instantly when a pan is hot enough to add a fresh fish fillet. A restaurant chef will know instinctively how to juggle several pans on the stove, preparing three or four dishes simultaneously with care, safety, accuracy, and consistency. And a restaurant chef can tell the doneness of a piece of meat or fish simply by the look of it, or with the slightest touch.

In addition to a solid knowledge of all aspects of how to cook, the skills needed to succeed in a restaurant kitchen include timing, focus, urgency, and planning.

## CULINARY JOBS THAT REQUIRE YOU TO COOK

The following descriptions detail various culinary jobs that require hands-on cooking (among other) skills. As you will see, there are a variety of these types of jobs. The culinary industry is so large and broad that, if you want to cook for a living, you are likely to find a good match for your interests and skills.

### Fine-Dining Restaurants

Upscale restaurants are often considered by chefs and cooks to be the best places to work. These restaurants tend to offer interesting and unusual foods on their menu and provide superior quality service in a tastefully decorated dining room. These establishments will employ experienced chefs and cooks who prepare the dishes from scratch using premium, high-cost ingredients. Kitchen staff will often include one or more chefs, several chefs de partie, a pastry baker, and prep cooks or assistant cooks.

If you are able to land an entry-level job at a fine-dining restaurant, it will give you valuable experience for your resume as well as the opportunity to learn from well-respected experienced chefs.

## Casual Dining Restaurants

Restaurants that offer casual dining often feature a limited number of easy-to-prepare items, supplemented by short-order specialities, and ready-made desserts. Often, one or two cooks prepare all of the food with the help of a short-order cook and one or two kitchen workers. Casual restaurants include most chain restaurants, family-style restaurants, and fast-food restaurants that offer a seating area.

## Catering

While offering much of the same adrenalin rush as restaurant work, catering provides a number of different options in a variety of work environments. If you love to plan parties and have a good sense of marketing (or come from a marketing background), catering may provide you with what you are looking for in the culinary world. Catering can be as varied as providing strawberry tarts for a 20-guest bridal shower to a full three-course dinner for a thousand-person banquet to receptions with wines for 300 people or more. Caterers are typically employed by the owners of banquet halls, reception halls, party rooms, and hotels that handle special events such as wedding receptions, holiday parties, bar or bat mitzvahs, sweet-sixteen parties, and corporate events.

Again, it is essential to consider the kind of work environment you would prefer. In the catering world, work is divided between prep and on site. Prep work is done in advance, usually in the catering company's own kitchens, and then transported to the event site for service. Prep work can involve making sauces and dressings, cutting vegetables, preparing fruits for desserts, even precooking elements of a meal to be reheated or put through the final cooking on site. While focus and the ability to work under pressure are certainly needed for prep work, the environment is generally not the same as what a chef de partie would experience in the middle of a dinner rush at a high-volume restaurant.

For on-site work, much of the responsibility involves reheating, plating, and serving. In some cases, the servers handle plating, but more often a caterer will bring a team to prep the food the servers will then distribute. On-site work can pay higher than prep work, and you might not have a daily 7 A.M. start time, as you might in restaurant work.

If you choose a smaller catering company, or even decide to start your own, your responsibilities will be far more varied and could require good business knowledge as well. You may find yourself cooking only 20% of your time, while the rest of your time is spent in developing menus for clients, marketing your services, or invoicing and billing. If you have defined your skill set as that of an entrepreneur but you still want to be in the kitchen, this may be an area for you to investigate.

## The Hospitality Industry: Hotels, Bed-and-Breakfasts, and Resorts

Hotel jobs can offer culinary graduates a range of varied opportunities. Hotel restaurants, cafés, and bars all offer jobs similar to those found in stand-alone restaurants. In addition to their on-site restaurants, nicer hotels will also offer room service. Many hotels also have a special event business that requires chefs, sous chefs, and line cooks to handle banquets, receptions, weddings, and corporate events. Besides the cooking line, hotels offer jobs in event management, booking, and marketing—all of which do not require hands-on cooking skills but rather strong business and interpersonal skills. We will discuss more of those opportunities in sections to come.

Working at a bed-and-breakfast is similar to working at a hotel, but typically on a smaller scale. Since many B&Bs are converted houses, they usually have fewer rooms, and thus fewer guests, than hotels. Running a B&B is not without its own challenges, however. Like many small businesses, B&B owners wear many hats and may undertake the building management, marketing, housekeeping, financials, and cooking all by themselves. Many B&Bs offer family-style meals, where all of the guests are invited to enjoy meals together. So it helps if the owners are personable and enjoy making conversation with their guests.

If your idea of a great career involves travel, the hospitality industry may be a good place to investigate. Opportunities abound to work for resorts internationally, letting you combine your love of cooking with a passion for exotic locations. For chefs, the hotel world can offer more regular hours than many restaurants and often more extensive health and insurance benefit packages. You may be able to find part-time or seasonal work at a popular tourist resort as a way to break into the field.

## Clubs

In addition to athletic and social country clubs, there are also private clubs, university clubs, and military clubs that serve meals, host special events, and offer catering services. The jobs available in clubs are similar to those described earlier in restaurants or in hotels. This is yet another avenue to consider when evaluating a culinary career. One benefit of working in clubs is that they can offer a variety of settings. For example, one Ivy League university in the Northeast offers eating clubs, where student members are served high-end meals year-round. Private and country clubs have locations nationwide and are often upscale properties. Military clubs (for example, an officer's club on a military base) will frequently hire civilians, are often located overseas, and provide candidates an opportunity to travel and live abroad.

## Food Retail

The past few years have seen tremendous growth in large-scale supermarkets nationwide. Most of these markets have extensive prepared-foods departments, which require a substantial staff to plan, develop, cook, and merchandise the food. These environments do not have the frenzied pace of some professional restaurant kitchens, so if you are looking for what you might consider a more manageable pace, this world may be for you. In addition, these jobs often require you to interact with the public, helping them make choices or offering general customer service. If you enjoy people and good interpersonal skills are a strong part of your skill set, you might want to investigate job opportunities here.

If you have ever dreamed of owning your own business, but have decided that running a full-service restaurant is not for you, you might want to look into joining or running your own specialty food business. You can decide whether you want to include a small café or a prepared-foods business as well, or just stick to stocking and selling merchandise. Either way, you experience the exciting challenge of sourcing products to sell, which can involve travel as well.

An enormous range of specialty food is stocked by stores today, from cheese shops and bakeries to shops selling varieties of charcuterie, meats, coffees, and teas, to oils, specialty salts, and herbs. Think about your favorite food and you can most likely find a specialty shop that sells it. Or start your own! Opportunities in specialty food retail usually require good people-management skills as well as good general business skills such as accounting, bookkeeping, and marketing, in addition to a solid knowledge of food. A small retail business might be a good place to look if you are thinking about using your culinary skills in a second career.

## Institutional Food Service

There is a large culinary world aside from restaurants. One area that can be more stable than the risky environment of a restaurant is the institutional food world. This includes hospitals, schools, and universities, as well as corporate cafeterias. Some corporations even have full-scale restaurants as a service to executives. Jobs in the institutional food world can range from preparing patients' trays in hospitals to preparing and serving food cafeteria style, with an emphasis on more fast-food related items such as sandwiches and burgers. While the volume can be high in some of these jobs, the hours can be more regular than in restaurants, hotels, catering, and even retail. Many institutes serve breakfast, so you might start at 6 A.M. and finish your shift by early afternoon. Often with these jobs, you can have evenings free, unlike the inevitable late nights in the restaurant world. This is one of the few culinary professions to offer a predictable schedule.

## Personal or Private Chef

One of the fastest-growing fields in culinary arts is that of personal chef. Personal or private chefs plan and create meals for individuals, couples, or entire families, usually in their clients' homes. Being a personal chef demands a solid knowledge of food, including a wide variety of recipes and menus, along with the self-motivation to market yourself to develop your client base.

Personal chefs use a number of business models. The most common one calls for the personal chef to visit the client weekly and prepare a range of meals to be refrigerated or frozen for use throughout the week. In some cases, a personal chef might be hired to come to clients on a periodic basis to prepare meals for dinner parties. A private chef, on the other hand, usually works full time for one client (and may even live on location) and is responsible for creating all meals for the client. A private chef generally handles all shopping and may be asked to serve the food as well.

Key skills needed in order to be a personal or private chef include an enjoyment of being around people, particularly children, since many jobs including preparing meals for families. In addition, good basic business skill is important, since most likely the chef does all of the invoicing and bookkeeping. A good sense of marketing can help, too: success depends on finding new clients or replacing ones who have left.

Being a personal chef can be a great career if you like working for yourself but do not want the overhead of running a larger business. You can often make your own hours and work as much or little as you like. It is definitely not for people who like a structured daily schedule. However, for those who like mobility as well as meeting people, being a personal chef can be a great small business.

Several new trends in the world of personal chefs are providing even more opportunities for culinary professionals. Clients who have dietary restrictions and do not cook or who choose not to prepare meals for themselves are hiring personal chefs. For someone who is diagnosed lactose intolerant or whose doctor has prescribed a gluten-free diet, for example, finding and using replacement ingredients can be daunting. Medical conditions, from cancer to heart problems, that require special diets can prompt a patient to hire a personal chef. You might consider becoming a specialist of particular diets, and seek out clients with those needs. This can be a way of differentiating yourself from the competition and helping to secure a client base.

Another growing trend is for personal chefs to teach cooking to clients in their homes. Many people who want to learn to cook do not feel comfortable going to public cooking classes. Teaching one or two people in their own home is a great way to build your teaching skills and offers something special to your clients. In addition, many chefs often do cooking parties—an evening or afternoon of several friends gathered to learn to cook and to eat the result!

## Health-Supportive Culinary Programs

Culinary programs specializing in natural, vegetarian, or raw foods are a good choice for those interested in food and health. Such programs sometimes offer wonderful opportunities for internships, for example, in spas and health resorts. See *Program Structure* in Chapter 3 for more information. Health-supportive programs are designed to emphasize nutrition theory and to teach the preparation of a wider variety of grains and legumes than other schools, as well as ways to minimize fats, sugars, and salt.

## Food Stylist and Food Photographer

If you have an art background or your skill set is strong in visual talents, you may want to consider becoming a food stylist. Food stylists create and prepare food for photography in magazines and books, in various forms of advertising, and on television. Food styling is a collaborative process between the stylist and the photographer; ideally, the stylist understands the principles of photography as well as basic design. The stylist's job is to make the food look its best on camera. Sometimes the food is completely cooked and prepared as if it were to be eaten, and sometimes it is not. Truth in advertising requires that if you are advertising ice cream, then you must use real ice cream. However, a food stylist has many tricks and techniques to make food look its best under the hot lights of a shoot and to continue to appear fresh after many long hours of shooting. A food stylist's kit often resembles a large makeup case, containing everything necessary to give a cosmetic makeover to the food being photographed. A solid knowledge of cooking techniques is essential here, as are the techniques used to make steam look as if it were continually rising from a chicken that came from the oven hours ago or a bowl of cereal look as if the milk has just been poured on.

Despite being one of most fascinating and better-paying areas of the culinary world, food styling can be one of the most difficult to get into. Few actual courses of study exist to prepare you for the job, and it takes years of experience in a variety of circumstances to learn the essential techniques of the trade. Most food stylists start as apprentices and assistants to more established professionals and work their way into their own careers.

If you have experience as a professional photographer, but thus far have not made food a specialty, you may want to consider building your career in this direction. Is photography your hobby? Take some additional design and photography courses to turn your amateur work into professional food photography credentials. Some photographers combine the disciplines, styling food as well as doing their own photography.

### Insider's Advice

*One of the key skills as a food stylist is diplomacy. Whether it is a magazine job or a cookbook photoshoot, there are a lot of people on the team, from art directors to food editors to authors and designers. Have a* can do *attitude. It is not always easy to make the food look and react as you want it to, particularly under hot studio lights, but that's ultimately what you are there to do.*

—Victoria Granof, food stylist, New York City

## Recipe Tester and Recipe Developer

The recipes in most good magazines, books, and websites are tested over and over again by a team of culinary professionals to make sure they will work in the average home kitchen. Even if the original recipes come from a trusted source, editors need to make sure that the measurements and timings in the recipes are correct.

Testing and developing are different jobs. Testing usually means a cook will prepare a recipe exactly as written to determine if any changes need to be made and will report his or her findings to an editor. A developer, on the other hand, actually tests a recipe a number of different ways and is constantly adjusting ingredients, amounts, and cooking times to make the recipe work and taste better.

Recipe testing can be a good way for a recent culinary graduate to begin in the food world, since all it really requires is a solid knowledge of cooking techniques and the ability to execute a recipe well. Developing requires more knowledge of food science and usually demands some time spent as an intern in a test kitchen, such as that of a magazine, a TV station, or even a food product company. A developer needs to know how to adjust ingredients and cooking techniques depending on often very strict parameters of calorie count and nutritional analysis. Many full-time recipe developers began their careers as recipe testers, showing that it is possible to move up.

## Cooking Instructor or Teacher

We are a good two generations past the era when families ate home-cooked meals as the norm and using prepared or prepacked food was the exception. In a new trend, more people want to learn to cook and return once again to the kitchen and make their own meals for their families and friends. Aside from pure economics, people are finding a sense of grounding and nurturing when they create their own food and can control the preparation and ingredients.

Interest in recreational cooking schools is gradually reviving. Students are looking to take cooking classes for fun, but also to learn basic cooking techniques that even their own mothers did not know. So, more than ever, being a cooking teacher is yet another viable option for today's culinary professional.

If your skills include teaching, public speaking, training, or coaching, a career as a culinary teacher may be a perfect fit for you. The job requires a great deal of research, planning, confidence speaking in front of a group, clear communication skills, and above all, patience. There are many great chefs, but as anyone who has watched the cooking shows on reality TV can attest, they do not always make great teachers. If you can communicate the techniques and processes of cooking clearly and effectively, whether in public classes or in private homes, you might decide that teaching is the career for you.

Some states require cooking teachers to be licensed, so be sure check with the department of education governing the area in which you would like to teach before applying for a position.

## CULINARY JOBS THAT DO NOT REQUIRE YOU TO COOK

While the vast majority of jobs in the culinary world do require you to spend some time in the kitchen, there are career paths and jobs that allow you to be around food without getting your hands spattered. If your background or interest is in general business management, there is a great deal of opportunity for you. Aside from cooks, restaurants need managers and accounting or marketing professionals, and there is whole range of front-of-house jobs from reservationists to hosts to special event coordinators to publicists.

### Food Writer

If you have always liked to write and have a gift for words, you may want to explore a career path as a cookbook writer, food writer, or restaurant reviewer. Many chefs decide, for promotional reasons, to have a cookbook published but may not be as comfortable delivering a manuscript as they would a braised veal shank. Often chefs need writers to assist them in translating their experience and the world of their kitchen into prose that makes sense, that cookbook readers will be able to understand. Often cookbooks include a chef's biography or a first-person story of their life in the industry.

As a freelance writer hired for a project, you may be called upon to interview the chef and then write those sections in his or her own voice. The same is true for many magazines who publish cookbooks under their own brand names. Often a team of freelance writers is assembled to assist the staff editors with the additional copy that frames a recipe (called the *headnote*) and supplements the recipes in the collection.

You may decide that your passion is to collect and write your own recipes and then publish a cookbook of your own. You will need to organize information logically so the reader can understand it, as well as write the headnotes with accuracy and personality. You will also need to find a publisher. Using a literary agent can help you navigate the world of publishing. Agents can help you to negotiate compensation, ensure that your vision is represented in the final text, and even make sure your publisher arranges for adequate publicity. Literally thousands of new cookbooks are published every year, so competition for sales is fierce. You will need to plan very carefully and be able to show what sets your cookbook apart from all the rest—what your *handle* is.

## Restaurant Reviewer

If you enjoy observation and critical writing, the role of restaurant reviewer may be for you. It is challenging to find full-time work reviewing; many culinary professionals combine reviewing and food feature writing with other jobs or related culinary careers.

It is more difficult than many people realize to write convincingly and vividly about food. A reviewer must be able to recreate the look, smell, and taste of a meal for readers. A good way to hone your food writing skills is to start a blog. Blogs are becoming one of the best ways for food professionals to connect with each other and write about their experiences. Writing a blog focusing on your own food experiences will help discipline you as well as give you practice in the craft of writing before you have to convince an employer to hire you as a food writer.

If you want to be a food writer, make sure you not only write as much as you can for practice, but also read as much as possible. Read a wide variety of classic food writers, such as M.F.K Fisher, Elizabeth David, and Richard Olney, as well as current ones.

## Culinary Product Representative

If your previous career was in marketing or sales, an easy transition to the culinary world could be as a culinary product sales representative or manager. Your culinary training can provide added depth and knowledge when you describe the products you are selling, and your existing background will give you the foundation to build your new career.

A job as a sales representative usually involves travel, so if you enjoy being on the road, either in your car or jetting around the country, this path may be for you. Excellent interpersonal skills, and comfort speaking in front of people is required. Whether you are selling food products or kitchen appliances, you may often be called upon to perform demonstrations in retail locations or with perspective buyers. If you are excited by running or managing your own business and have a strong entrepreneurial sense, a career in product sales could be a great path.

## Nutrition and Food Science

Perhaps you enjoy science and those labs were among your favorite courses in high school or college. You may want to investigate becoming a registered dietician or nutritionist or even enter the dynamic field of food research and development. Rather than a regular culinary school diploma, a registered dietician needs special schooling in the fields of biology and chemistry as well as psychology. A culinary degree is certainly helpful since a registered dietician counsels clients on a daily basis on how to revise their eating habits. The added skill of being able to suggest culinary preparations, recipes, and tips may give you a competitive edge in finding a job if you have a culinary diploma as well as the added coursework and certification needed in the dietician field.

Food research and development involves testing and creating new flavors, tastes, and even new products. Opportunities are usually with large commercial food companies and can involve much hands-on cooking, creating, and testing new food preparations. Consider programs or additional schooling that focuses more on culinary science than the more common career programs designed to prepare you for a job as a restaurant sous chef.

## The Business of Food: Finance, Accounting, Marketing, and Public Relations

You may decide that while you are passionate about the food world and enjoy cooking, you do not want hands-on food experience to be a part of your job. The good news is that there are many opportunities in the business side of the food industry. If you are a career changer with a specialty in accounting, why not take a few recreational cooking classes to familiarize yourself with terms and methods, and then bring your years of previous experience to a finance role with a major restaurant or food chain?

Many other roles in food businesses do not demand that you be involved as an active cook. All restaurants and most chefs could use a bit of public relations (PR) and marketing to help their businesses grow. The marketing world is another area that is ideal for career changers if you bring some experience. It can also offer some opportunity if you are just starting out. Gaining the consumer's attention is more difficult than ever before, but more and more smart marketers are taking advantage of the variety of social media to communicate their messages.

In these career roles, you may not need a full culinary degree but rather an intensive recreational course covering the basics. Even if you do not plan to become a professional chef, knowing the basics of good cooking and cuisine will help you in any career in the food industry outside the kitchen.

You might also want to look into culinary management programs offered by business schools as well as culinary schools. These programs focus on honing your skills in operating and managing a culinary-based business. Developing and executing business plans, hiring and training staff, the economics of maintaining a business, and the basics of marketing and PR are essential parts of these programs.

## Food Media: Television and Internet

There is no question that the world of television has become an enormous influence in the promotion of food. Full-time food-related programming appears not only on dedicated networks, but national networks now include shows dedicated to food. (And increasingly, the footage is also viewed on the Internet.) If you are interested in the dynamic world of media, television has a lot to offer. Food television requires actual cooks, people to prepare food for the camera, handle the prep work, and assist the on-air talent as well as test and develop recipes to be used on a show. Writers, editors, film crews, set designers, wardrobe and makeup assistants, as well as a fleet of administrative workers, are required to create food shows. Such unexpected roles as librarian and fact checker, as well as producer, writer, and script developer, are often a source of opportunity.

A great deal of competition exists for television food jobs; the best way to get your foot in the door is to work as an unpaid intern. An internship is part of many culinary academic programs, so if you are interested in television, use your internship to gain experience and a competitive edge.

With such numerous and diverse opportunities, there is bound to be a culinary career just right for you!

# CHAPTER three

## CULINARY TRAINING: DIPLOMAS, DEGREES, AND CERTIFICATES

**ONCE YOU** have decided to pursue a culinary career, established your skill set, and envisioned the sector of the food world in which you would like to work, the next step is to think about your culinary education and find out where to get the training to qualify for the job of your choice.

Culinary employment can demand a formal culinary diploma, require any of a wide variety of training certificates, or be solely dependent on your display of hands-on skill in an on-premises kitchen interview. For restaurant positions in higher-end establishments, a hiring chef will probably want to see a culinary degree from an accredited school and some form of internship experience before offering you a position.

## PREREQUISITES

If you have not yet completed high school, you can start taking courses that will help you prepare to enter the culinary arts field. First of all, make sure that you have a handle on the basic skills such as reading comprehension, writing, computer literacy, and basic mathematics. Then, ask your guidance counselor or home economics instructor whether your high school offers any specialized training programs. One example is the Careers through Culinary Arts Program (CCAP). Founded in 1990 in New York City, this program allows high school students to obtain practical training. At the end of the program, each student may enter a cooking contest and compete for scholarships to post-secondary culinary schools. This program is available in seven states and helps more than 12,000 students annually to enter the field of culinary arts. See Appendix C for contact information for this program.

## CERTIFICATION ORGANIZATIONS

The American Culinary Federation Foundation Accrediting Commission (ACFFAC) currently accredits more than 165 culinary training programs in the United States. Completion of these programs can lead to an associate's degree, certificate, or diploma in the culinary arts (see Appendix D). We will discuss the options of various programs in this chapter.

> There are no national certification examinations for work in the culinary arts. The most common certification—for *food handler safety*—is made by the individual states. However, individual organizations and schools offer various certifications that can help you improve your skills for culinary related positions.

Many state and local regulatory food-protection agencies have mandated some form of certification for food handlers. This requirement is most often related to food safety. As these conditions vary from state to state, it is important for you to be aware of the guidelines in the state where you plan to work.

The following is a list of national organizations that provide various examinations and certificates. These certifications may or may not be necessary or useful for you and your career progression. Check with others in your chosen area and in your local state before pursuing any certification.

## The Culinary Institute of America

The Culinary Institute of America (CIA) offers culinary certification at three levels in the areas of culinary arts, personnel management, and financial administration. After completing each level, candidates receive certificates from the CIA and ACF. See www.ciaprochef.com/prochef/ for more information.

## The National Registry

The National Registry of Food Safety Professionals (NRFSP) certification is accredited by the American National Standards Institute using standards set by the Conference for Food Protection. The National Registry's exam is accepted in all states and jurisdictions that recognize those standards. The site offers Food Safety Training Requirements by state and an overview of exam questions. For more information go to www.nrfsp.com/.

## The American Culinary Federation

The American Culinary Federation (ACF) offers 14 certification designations, each requiring specific qualifications in the area of cooking professionals, personal cooking professionals, baking and pastry professionals, culinary administrators, and educators. For more information go to www.acfchefs.org/. See Appendix D for a list of the ACF certifications.

## The National Restaurant Association

The National Restaurant Association (NRA) offers a wide range of food-related resources and information on certification programs at www.restaurant.org/. For information on the Foodservice Management Professional® (FMP®) credential, see http://managefirst.restaurant.org/fmp/.

## EVALUATING CULINARY PROGRAMS

As we learned in Chapter 1, there are many types of positions available in the culinary world. Correspondingly, there are varied training programs to help candidates prepare for these jobs. While some offer general culinary training, others are designed to teach you to master a specific skill. It is important for you to do your research in order to decide which program is the best fit for your interests and needs. One of the most important decisions for aspiring culinary professionals is determining what type of position you ultimately want to have. Once you have determined this, you can work backwards to consider the kind of degree or certification you need in order to achieve your specific culinary career goals. The answer may surprise you. A shorter program may give you the training you need, which means you might not need to seek a full professional certification.

Generally, programs can be divided into two categories:

1. professional diploma programs and culinary degrees awarded by dedicated culinary schools, universities, and community colleges, and
2. nonprofessional certificate programs awarded by a wide variety of schools and institutes.

Like any other professional field, culinary training can sometimes be both lengthy and expensive. To avoid spending time and money unnecessarily, you should be sure you are committed to a particular path before entering into a program. Many culinary professionals start by working as a server in restaurant or as an apprentice. Once they have had a chance to experience the daily realities of working in the culinary field, they embark on a formal training program.

### Insider's Advice

*I discovered that there are certificate programs offered by all kinds of schools. I did an eight-month Saturday program at the French Culinary Institute before I decided to take the plunge and do a full-time, six-month diploma program at the Institute of Culinary Education. Schools decide whether to consider programs worthy of a professional credential depending on the number of hours required and how in depth they are.*

—A culinary professional

If your goal is to begin your work in a well-known, respected restaurant, it may be best for you to pursue a culinary degree. Although it is certainly true that there are workers in restaurants who have never attended a culinary school, from an executive chef's point of view, a culinary degree will certainly make you stand out. Having a degree is an indication of the experience you have had and suggests the quality of what you may be able to contribute to an employer.

### Insider's Advice

*Don't be discouraged if you aren't able to get a culinary degree or diploma or even a certificate from an esteemed cooking school. If you are comfortable in a professional kitchen, if you take orders well, if you learn quickly you can stand out as a restaurant worker. The degree does not 100% indicate what the pros call kitchen smarts!*

—A culinary professional

If you are more interested in institutional cooking, corporate food service, or even retail food work, less expensive and less time-consuming programs might amply serve your needs. If, for example, you are a career changer and already possess an established skill set, yet need training in the basics of food preparation, many nonprofessional certification programs can give you what you need to enter the area of the industry you choose.

No matter where you live or what your budget, chances are good that you will be able to find solid training for a culinary arts career. Schools often have some form of financial aid and loans. There are many options to choose from, and the choice comes down to how much time you want to devote to your training and how much money you are able to spend on or borrow for your culinary education. But do consider other factors, such as the depth of content a program offers and how it will help you refine or develop your skills for your new career.

## The Time Factor

Though programs vary widely, a complete diploma program from an accredited culinary school requires about six months of full-time attendance. Classes normally meet Monday through Friday, either in the morning or the afternoon. If you cannot manage a full-time program, there are usually opportunities to attend classes in the evening several nights a week or only on weekends or a combination of the two. In this case, your training might stretch out to nine months or longer. This could work to your advantage, however, because such a schedule allows you to work at least a part-time job while you are attending culinary classes. When deciding between full- and part-time study, be sure to consider whether or not you are financially able to support yourself.

If you decide you want to pursue a formal training program such as that offered by the well-respected Culinary Institute of America, you will have a much longer time commitment. The CIA's Bachelor of Professional Studies program takes a total of 38 months to complete. This is a comprehensive program focusing on both theory and practice. Graduating from this type of program will often help candidates land more prestigious positions and earn higher salaries. On average, those who graduate with a bachelors degree (in any field) will earn over $1 million more than their counterparts in the same field without a degree. This is another key consideration when choosing the type of program you wish to pursue.

## The Cost

Culinary training can cost as little as several hundred dollars for nonprofessional certifications to well over $40,000 for longer-term diploma programs.

Nonprofessional certifications are usually designed for serious home cooks; they are shorter and less in depth than certificate programs. Designed to give an overview of culinary procedures, they do not include the training in timing and speed that full professional programs provide. They can be a good introduction to culinary arts if you want to test out your desire for a culinary career before you commit to a longer-term, more expensive certificate program or a multiyear diploma program.

Loan and financial aid opportunities are available through most culinary programs. In fact, many schools offer work-study options, which allow you to work at your school while you are earning credits toward your tuition. Each school you are considering can advise you best on its financial assistance programs. Often, financial aid information is posted on the school's website, or you can call and speak with a financial aid counselor. Besides the school's location, tuition, reputation, and courses offered, the amount of financial aid offered to accepted students is frequently one of the most important considerations when choosing the right program.

## The Advantage of a Varied Program

A good way to evaluate a program is to see how intensively the program will allow you to gain experience in a variety of international cuisines. Most programs are based in classic French technique, but a grounding in this solid technique enables you to execute a variety of cuisines—and is what will most likely get you a job.

Once you have worked a bit with international cooking, many programs shift their focus and begin to train you in the basics of baking and pastry. You will learn the basics of doughs, yeasts, breads, cakes, pies, and chocolate in addition to techniques in the construction and plating of desserts.

If you are following a course designed to prepare you for the restaurant world, your chef-instructor may start to introduce the idea of timed preparation of food. Often at this part in your training, you may be given a series of dishes to prepare, with a set time in which they must be finished, plated, and presented to your chef for inspection. This is the beginning of training you for the world of the restaurant, where your skills in timing and working on multiple dishes simultaneously must be exact.

In addition, you most likely will begin to be exposed to the principles of culinary business management. Some programs offer substantial credit hours devoted to the mechanics of running a restaurant, hiring and training staff, basic restaurant accounting and marketing, and ordering inventory.

## PROGRAM STRUCTURE

To help you decide what you need, let us take a look at how most programs are structured. Degrees, diplomas, and certificates differ essentially in three ways:

1. the amount of time spent in the classroom,
2. the range of food-related subjects covered and tested, and
3. how broad and deep the instruction takes you into the world of food.

A professional diploma program typically requires around 600 hours of culinary classroom instruction, with frequent tests and hands-on examinations. A nonprofessional certificate program can be intensive but require only 100 hours, with no formal examinations. We will take another look at these later, but let us start with the areas most programs have in common.

Most programs begin with a **basic introduction to the kitchen**. Pots, pans, and utensils are identified and their uses are discussed. Following that, you might begin an extensive training in ingredients and their properties. You will learn fruits and vegetables, dairy products, and herbs and spices. These will be your building blocks in the kitchen, and even if you think you know something about them, there are many properties of even common ingredients that might surprise you.

You will certainly be introduced to the **principles of food sanitation and safety**. This is a tremendously important area in training a culinary professional at any level. All states have strict requirements that accredited diploma programs cover this material and that all students be tested on their knowledge. Should you decide to pursue a nonprofessional certification, you can find further courses on food safety training to obtain a marketable level of training.

At some point early on in any training, you will be introduced to **knife skills**. No matter where you go in the industry, if your job includes hands-on food preparation, it will be imperative that you learn and master good solid knife skills. Unlike home cooks, food professionals need to be efficient in volume and speed. In other words, they need to prepare large amounts of food quickly and without waste. Good knife skills are essential to accomplish this.

Your training then will the mostly likely move to an intensive understanding of **cooking preparations and techniques**. You may work alone or in teams, but most often your training will consist of demonstrations by a chef, followed by your own opportunity to prepare a variety of dishes that will then be critiqued by your chef-instructor. You will learn and develop the skills of roasting, sautéing, frying, grilling, poaching, steaming, braising, and stewing, from vegetables to meats and fish, all accompanied by classic dishes chosen to demonstrate and make you familiar with those techniques.

As you near the end of your basic training, you most likely will encounter some good **hands-on experience** in a restaurant or training kitchen. For example, the Institute of Culinary Education in New York City provides a final module of practical experience, usually in local restaurants, for students who have completed five modules of training. The French Culinary Institute, also in New York City, has its own student-run commercial restaurant on the premises. Here, students hone their skills while exposed to the realities and pace of a professional kitchen and cooking for paying customers.

If you have chosen a nonprofessional certification program, your training may end here. Even though you have only a certificate of completion and acceptable attendance, this may be enough to qualify you to pursue jobs in food media, styling, or retail kitchen work.

If you choose a longer, more intensive diploma or degree program, your program will mostly like continue and include a deeper exploration of a variety of cuisines. Once you have mastered key cooking techniques and principles, you will gain an understanding of international ethnic cuisines such as classic French and Italian, but also Asian and Latin techniques, ingredients, and dishes.

**Insider's Advice**

Who:      Alex Darvishi, CEC, AAC
             (Certified Executive Chef, American Academy of
             Chefs)

What:      Executive Chef at Meridian Hills Country Club

Where:    Indianapolis, Indiana

How Long: 30+ years in the culinary arts field

*It is a good idea to call a few places and ask if you can observe their kitchen before you decide to enter the culinary arts field. Doing so will help you face the reality of the long hours and hard work needed in this career. In addition, visit a few culinary schools and speak to some of the students about their program.*

*If you decide a culinary career is right for you, a good path to take is to become an apprentice for three years to get the real-world experience that you need and then enroll in a culinary school. During an apprenticeship, you get hands-on experience by going through all the different stations in the kitchen. With this firm foundation in place, you will be able to absorb and understand more while in culinary school. After completing a culinary program, it takes many years of hard work and diligence to become a chef. Don't expect to graduate from high school, go directly into a two-year culinary training program, and come out as a chef.*

*The first thing to learn about cooking is the importance of the basics. Don't be one of those people who skips through the basics in a hurry to get to the more fancy aspects of cooking. For example, you should know how to properly braise meat for a basic pot roast—many cooks, and even some chefs, do not know how to do this basic task. First get a firm grasp of the basics, then you can branch out and do more advanced work.*

## Sample Course Description

The following example gives a course description for a typical culinary degree program. It is from the associate of science program at the Art Institute of California (AIC) in Los Angeles (www.artinstitutes.edu/losangeles). Other programs are similar, but this progression of classes mirrors what is described in the text. Most programs—whether degree, diploma, or professional certificate—offer a version of this, but each school will have its own requirements.

## Graduation Requirements

To receive an associate of science degree in culinary arts from the Art Institute of California, students must complete a minimum of 112 quarter credits with a cumulative GPA of 2.0 or higher. The curriculum includes 112 credit hours and is typically completed in seven quarters.

## Sample Required Courses

### Concepts and Theories of Culinary Techniques

The fundamental concepts, skills, and techniques involved in basic cookery are covered in this course. Special emphasis is given to the study of ingredients and cooking theories. Lectures teach organization skills in the kitchen and work coordination. The basics of stocks, soups, sauces, vegetable cookery, starch cookery, meat, and poultry are covered. Emphasis is given to basic cooking techniques such as sautéing, roasting, poaching, braising, and frying.

### Introduction to Culinary Skills

Concepts, skills, and techniques of basic cooking are covered in the course. Lectures and demonstrations teach organization skills in the kitchen, work coordination, and knife skills. Emphasis is given to basic cooking techniques such as sautéing, roasting, poaching, braising, and frying. Students must successfully pass a practical cooking examination covering a variety of cooking techniques.

### Sanitation and Safety

This course is an introduction to food environmental sanitation and safety in a food production area. Attention is focused on food-borne illness and their origins, and on basic safety procedures followed in the foodservice industry. This was approved by the Federal Food and Drug Administration (FDA) and is recognized by 95% of state and local jurisdictions that require training or certification.

### Classical Cuisine

This is an in-depth study of the cuisine of the European continent. Advanced hands-on techniques will be utilized in the production of classical cuisine menus. Studies will be required on the foundation of cooking and the chefs associated with the development of Classical Cuisine as we know it today. A historical hands-on application will be emphasized in the cuisines of Escoffier, Carême, Verge, Bocuse, and others. Cultural implications in the preparation of foods and the selection of menus will be emphasized. Plate presentation, mise en place, organization, and utilizing the fundamental techniques of cooking will be reinforced at all times.

### International Cuisine

This course provides an in-depth study of the cuisine of South America, Australia, Africa, the Middle East, Scandinavia, Eastern Europe, and Asia. Advanced hands-on techniques will be utilized in the production of international cuisine menus. Studies will be required for products and ingredients that are indigenous to the various regions. Cultural implications in the preparation of foods and the selection of menus will be emphasized. Plate presentation, mise en place, organization, and utilizing the fundamental techniques of cooking will be reinforced at all times.

### Asian Cuisine

This course emphasizes both the influences and ingredients that create the unique character of selected Asian cuisines. Students prepare, taste, serve, and evaluate traditional regional dishes of China, Japan, Korea, Vietnam, Thailand, and Indonesia. Importance will be placed on ingredients, flavor profiles, preparations, and techniques representative of these cuisines.

### Regional Cuisine

This course provides students with a study of the cuisine of the region in the distinct locale of the school or city nearest to the school. Students learn about the products and ingredients that are indigenous to the region and gain hands-on experience preparing foods. A historical approach with cultural implications in the preparation of foods and the selection of menus will be stressed. Plate presentation, mise en place, organization, and utilizing the fundamental techniques of cooking will be reinforced at all times.

### American Regional Cuisine

The course reinforces the knowledge and skills learned in the preceding classes and helps students build confidence in the techniques of basic cookery. The development of knife skills is accented. American Regional Cuisine explores the use of indigenous ingredients in the preparation of traditional and contemporary American specialties. The concepts of mise en place, time lines, plate presentation, and teamwork in a production setting are introduced and accentuated. Timing and organization skills are emphasized.

## Purchasing and Product Identification

This course is a collaborative exploration of basic principles of purchasing food, equipment, and supplies. Primary focus is on product identification, supplier selection, and the ordering, receiving, storing, and issuing process.

## Management, Supervision, and Career Development

This course focuses on managing people from the hospitality supervisor's viewpoint. The emphasis is on techniques for increasing productivity, controlling labor costs, time management, and managing change. It also stresses effective communication and explains the responsibilities of a supervisor in the food service operation. Students develop techniques and strategies for marketing themselves in their chosen fields. Emphasis will be placed on students' assessing their more marketable skills, developing a network of contacts, generating interviews, writing cover letters and resumes, preparing for their employment interview, developing a professional appearance, closing, and follow-up.

## Introduction to Baking Science and Theory

Students are introduced to the fundamental concepts, skills, and techniques of baking. Special significance is placed on the study of ingredient functions, product identification, and weights and measures as applied to baking. Through lectures, demonstrations, production, tasting and testing, students learn yeast-raised dough mixing methods, pie dough, quick dough, cookie dough, and product finishing techniques. Students must pass a practical exam.

## Garde Manger

This course provides students with skills and knowledge of the organization, equipment and responsibilities of the garde manger, or *cold kitchen*. Students are introduced to and prepare cold hors d'oeuvres, sandwiches, and salads, as well as basic charcuterie items while focusing on the total utilization of product. Reception foods and buffet arrangements are introduced. Students must pass a written and practical exam.

## Externship

This course has been designed to acquaint the student with actual working conditions in an approved restaurant/hospitality establishment. This course is a supervised entry-level work experience in the restaurant/hospitality field requiring a minimum of 90 work hours. Individual conferences and class attendance are required. Students are responsible for securing an externship job and may seek assistance through The Institute. Students gain experience needed to enter their field on graduation.

## CHOOSING THE RIGHT PROGRAM

In choosing a general culinary program, start to think about which area you might like best to work in. If you are a fascinated and passionate baker, there are certificate programs that only teach baking and pastry skills. They tend to be a bit less expensive than other certificate culinary programs and are shorter in time commitment as well. Most culinary programs do include at least a minimum of credit hours exposing you to baking and pastry skills, but if this is an area you really want to explore, it would be a good idea to focus on the pastry-only programs most schools offer. If culinary business management is your particular area of interest, explore programs that focus solely on this. Your training will not be hands-on cooking, but rather marketing and business theory and practice. Other areas to consider in evaluating programs include exposure to nutrition and hospitality management.

If you are just out of high school and serious about a culinary career, you may want to consider some of the two-year associate programs offered at community colleges. In addition to preparing you in the culinary arts, these courses can offer a general college curriculum including humanities, arts, and sciences courses. Some programs even offer basic computer training.

In general, remember that a longer program may not necessarily be the best one for you. Keep your eye on your ultimate goal of where you would like to be working and what you would like to be doing. Culinary training is very different from attending a liberal arts college where you might not really know where you want to go in life as you pursue your studies. If you have a sense of how you would like to apply your culinary knowledge and skills at the outset, as you choose your program, you will be able to make a wise decision and find opportunities that will best prepare you for your first jobs.

If you know culinary training is for you, but remain unsure of what you want to do afterwards, relax. Most students change their mind about what they want to do after they finish their program. What is important is that you explore as many possibilities as you can while still in school. Remain open and flexible.

## ATTAINING A HEALTH CERTIFICATE

Health certificates for food handlers and foodservice managers are mandated by jurisdictions in each county, city, or state. Therefore, you should be aware of the laws in the area in which you are seeking employment. In many states, it is only necessary for one person on staff in a kitchen facility to hold food-safety certification. Much depends on the type of kitchen facility, however, for in institutional cooking environments—hospitals, school cafeterias, corporate dining rooms—every employee may need food-handling certification. The facility at which you seek employment will know the requirements. Be sure to ask, and if you already have food-handling certification, be sure to include it on your resume.

Attaining a food-handler certification is relatively simple. You sign up for and take a short course and exam, often online, to receive certification. The practice test questions in Skill Set 3: Food Safety and Proper Food Handling in Chapter 4 should prepare you for almost any food-handler certification exam, but it is still a good idea to review your state's specific guidelines online. In addition to information on where and when to take the certification exam, the website will often provide preparation materials for your review.

You can find your state or county's specific food safety requirements by visiting your local department of health's website or you can visit the following website:

www.foodsafetyinstituteofamerica.com/

A national food-safety training program called ServSafe is sponsored by the Educational Foundation of the National Restaurant Association. If you enroll in and pass this certification process, you will be granted a ServSafe certificate that is accepted in 95% of the jurisdictions across the nation. ServSafe courses may be offered by a culinary school or the local health department, or directly from the Educational Foundation of the National

Restaurant Association. You can learn more about this program at: www.servsafe.com/FoodSafety/.

Many culinary schools include a course or seminar on food safety and sanitation, in which you earn your area's health certificate or a ServSafe certificate. If you earn a local health certificate and then move to work in a different area, you will need to find out whether the new location will honor it. Again, contact the local health department for the answer. Getting all this information may seem daunting, but it is just one more step in a successful job search.

The following websites offer online content for food safety:

### National Registry for Food Safety Professionals

The National Registry for Food Safety Professionals offers state-specific food safety requirements, information for those who take and administer food safety exams, consumer information, news updates, and so on, at www.nrfsp.com/index.php/.

### Premier Food Safety

Premier Food Safety is a site that offers online food certification training for food handlers designed to teach students food safety concepts and prepare them to take the food-handler/manager certification exam. See http://premierfoodsafety.com/public/.

### Prometric Testing

Prometric Testing offers various food-related tests and assessments related to food safety training and certification. Accredited by the American National Standards Institute using standards set by the Conference for Food Protection, the site offers a wide variety of content and programs at www.experioronline.com/foodsafety/default.htm.

Again, be sure you are aware of the state requirements for the state where you plan to work before making decisions about enrolling in a training program or applying for a position.

# CHAPTER four

**THE FOLLOWING** questions are typical of those you would find on tests at a culinary institution or on a certification exam. These tests cover a wide range of skills and topics and are designed to help you prepare for the types of subjects you will learn and be tested on in culinary school. They include basic knowledge of topics as well as terms and techniques in a wide variety of culinary arts–related skills.

Although actual culinary exams vary widely, it is possible to group the questions into categories, or skill sets. Below are two practice tests. Each is divided into the five key skill sets you will encounter in any culinary training program:

1.  Basic Culinary Concepts and Methods
2.  Core Competencies
3.  Food Safety and Proper Food Handling
4.  Principles of Plating
5.  Organization of a Professional Kitchen

Answers to the two practice tests are provided in Appendix E.

## PRACTICE TEST 1

### Skill Set 1: Basic Culinary Concepts and Methods

#### Baking Skills

1.  Baking is the process of cooking food for _____ periods of time using _____ heat.
    a. short, direct
    b. long, dry
    c. short, moist
    d. long, direct

2.  Which best describes baking yeast?
    a. a dead organism that gives the dough color and taste
    b. a spice added to the dough that enhances its flavor and texture
    c. a living organism added to dough that aids the fermentation and rising process
    d. a type of salt that can be used in baking

3.  **True or False.** Salt should never be added to bread.

4.  Generally speaking, when a recipe calls for baking soda, what else can you expect to find in the recipe?
    a. an acidic ingredient
    b. salt
    c. a savory ingredient
    d. a bitter ingredient

5.  **True or False.** Layers of cold butter and dough make up the main parts of puff pastry.

6.  Generally speaking, when should you use baking powder?
    a. when baking bread
    b. when baking pastry
    c. when baking cookies
    d. when baking cakes

7.  Generally speaking, when should you use baking soda?
    a. when baking bread
    b. when baking pastry
    c. when baking cookies
    d. when baking cakes

8.  Yeast is mixed with what to activate it?
    a. water or milk
    b. egg
    c. butter
    d. dough

9.  Letting dough rest and rise is known as what?
    a. relaxing the dough
    b. proofing
    c. rising
    d. kneading

10. Which of the following is an example of yeast bread?
    a. French baguette
    b. sourdough
    c. challah
    d. all the above

### Braising Skills

11. Which of the following best describes braising?
    a. a tender cut of meat, fish, or poultry first seared in fat, then slow-cooked in a flavorful liquid
    b. a tough cut of meat, fish, or poultry first seared in fat, then slow-cooked in a flavorful liquid
    c. a large piece of meat, fish, or poultry slow-cooked in its own juices
    d. small bite-sized pieces of meat, fish, or poultry slow-cooked in a flavorful liquid

12. Complete the following sentence. Braising is a _____
    a. combination cooking method.
    b. single cooking method.
    c. relatively new cooking method.
    d. direct cooking method.

13. What are some characteristics of meats, fish, or poultry suited for braising?
    a. meat from a well-exercised part of the animal
    b. tender cut
    c. bite-sized
    d. thick

14. Braising meats breaks down what tough connective tissue of meat?
    a. fat
    b. ligaments
    c. collagen
    d. skin

15. The liquid used for braises can be made of which of the following?
    a. red wine
    b. stock
    c. fruit juice
    d. all of the above

16. The amount of liquid used while braising should _____
    a. cover the food completely.
    b. cover the food by one third to one half.
    c. cover the food by two thirds.
    d. cover the food by one quarter.

17. Mirepoix is usually added to braised items. Mirepoix is made up of what mixture of 3 vegetables?
    a. 2 parts onions, 1 part garlic, 1 part green pepper
    b. 2 parts onions, 1 part carrots, 1 part celery
    c. 1 part carrots, 1 part green peppers, 1 part garlic
    d. 2 parts garlic, 1 part onion, 1 part celery

18. Braising is generally done where?
    a. on the stovetop
    b. in the oven
    c. on the stove top and in the oven
    d. in a crockpot

19. _____ is the desired degree of doneness for braised foods.
    a. Shredded
    b. Medium rare
    c. Fork tender
    d. Well done

20. _____ is a cut of beef NOT suited for braising.
    a. Shoulder
    b. Brisket
    c. Shank
    d. Tenderloin

**Grilling Skills**

21. Which of the following is NOT a method for enhancing the flavor of grilled food?
    a. drying out food before cooking
    b. using a fresh spice rub
    c. presalting the food
    d. marinating the food overnight

22. Of the following, which is not well suited to grilling?
    a. fillet of tuna
    b. pork ribs
    c. a thin cut of flank steak
    d. a whole chicken

23. **True or False.** Grilling is best for tender, thinner cuts of meat or fish.

24. Which of the following is not a source of fuel for grilling?
    a. charcoal
    b. gas
    c. electric
    d. water

25. A grill _____ or _____ has ridges and is used on the stove top to simulate outdoor grilling indoors.
    a. pan, skillet
    b. tong, chips
    c. basket, skewer
    d. pan, basket

26. **True or False.** When cooking on a grill, various parts get hotter than others.

27. Grilling is a good method of cooking for _____ and _____.
    a. thick cuts of meat, whole chickens
    b. vegetables, tender cuts of meat and poultry
    c. vegetables, whole game
    d. thin cuts of meat, thick pieces of fish

28. Foods grilled outdoors often have a _____ flavor.
    a. buttery
    b. salty
    c. charred
    d. sweet

28. Grilled food is typically cooked _____
    a. slowly.
    b. quickly.
    c. when cold.
    d. when preheated.

30. Marinades are typically made up of oils, acids, and _____
    a. lime juice.
    b. sugar.
    c. olives.
    d. flour.

## Pastry Skills

31. Puff pastry, croissant, and Danish are examples of what kind of dough?
    a. laminated
    b. sugar
    c. gluten
    d. none of the above

32. The best flour for making pastry is _____
    a. soft wheat.
    b. whole wheat.
    c. rye.
    d. all-purpose.

33. Pie dough, muffins, and biscuits are best made using _____
    a. soft wheat flour.
    b. whole wheat flour.
    c. rye flour.
    d. all-purpose flour.

34. **True or False.** Layers of cold butter and dough make up the main parts of puff pastry.

35. Which of the following is a common ingredient in pastry dough?
    a. flour
    b. fat
    c. eggs
    d. all of the above

36. Which of the following is a factor in making a pastry dough or batter?
    a. proportion of the ingredients
    b. flavoring added
    c. mixing method used
    d. all of the above

37. What is another name for the rubbed dough method?
    a. smoothed dough method
    b. spread dough method
    c. cutting in method
    d. chopping in method

38. Which of the following is a description of the cutting in method?
    a. Ingredients are blended into a smooth batter.
    b. Chilled fat ingredient is rubbed into the flour to create flakes.
    c. Dry and wet ingredients are blended separately and then combined.
    d. none of the above

39. The purpose of the rubbed dough method is to _____
    a. produce a shiny pastry when food is baked.
    b. produce a tender flaky food when baked.
    c. produce a small pastry that is bite sized.
    d. produce a fruit or vegetable filled pastry to be served as an appetizer.

## Poaching Skills

40. What are the two types of poaching?
    a. high, low
    b. deep, shallow
    c. small, large
    d. full, half

41. What kind of cooking technique is poaching?
    a. moist
    b. old
    c. new
    d. traditional

42. When poaching, foods should be _____ submerged in a heated liquid.
    a. partially
    b. completely
    c. both **a** and **b**
    d. none of above

**43.** Poaching is generally reserved for naturally _____ foods.
a. tender
b. tough
c. small
d. large

**44.** An appropriate food for poaching would be _____
a. lobster.
b. young birds.
c. shrimp.
d. all of the above

**45.** Which best describes deep poaching?
a. completely submerging an item in a liquid kept at a constant moderate temperature
b. partially submerging an item in a liquid kept at a constant high temperature
c. completely submerging an item in a liquid kept at a constant high temperature
d. partially submerging an item in a liquid kept at a constant moderate temperature

### Roasting Skills

To answer questions 46 and 47, choose the correct definition of the underlined word.

**46.** The duck was <u>roasted</u> to perfection.
a. cooked in the oven by indirect heat
b. cooked over coals
c. cooked with salt
d. cooked in water

47. To add flavor to the figs the chef <u>barded</u> them.
    a. sautéed them in butter
    b. tied strips of bacon around them
    c. placed them on a piece of parchment paper
    d. chilled them

48. **True or False.** Larding can help add food flavor to a food.

49. A roasting pan should have a _____ bottom with _____ sides.
    a. curved, high
    b. uneven, high
    c. flat, low
    d. flat, high

50. **True or False.** When roasting, the pan should be covered.

51. Roasting is most similar to which of the following styles of cooking?
    a. baking
    b. toasting
    c. grilling
    d. frying

52. Many roasted foods are _____ before cooking.
    a. stuffed
    b. seasoned
    c. both **a** and **b**
    d. none of the above

### Sauce-Making Skills

53. What are some common purposes of adding a sauce to a dish?
    a. to add moisture
    b. to add texture
    c. to add flavor
    d. all of the above

54. Traditionally, how many *mother* sauces are there?
    a. 6
    b. 5
    c. 4
    d. 3

55. Generally speaking, for making batches of a sauce base, the type of pot or pan necessary is a _____
    a. fry pan.
    b. sauce pot.
    c. stock pot.
    d. saucier.

56. The mother sauces are espagnole, béchamel, velouté, _____, and _____.
    a. tomato, hollandaise
    b. ketchup, mayonnaise
    c. jus de veau lié, demi glace
    d. none of the above

57. What equipment may be necessary for preparing a sauce?
    a. tasting spoon, strainer
    b. thermometer, gloves
    c. eye protection, splatter screen
    d. tongs, strainer

58. To pince tomato paste is to do what?
    a. brown the paste
    b. add butter to the paste
    c. thicken the paste
    d. cook the paste down

59. The purpose of pince is to _____ the paste's acidity and _____ flavor to the sauce.
    a. reduce, add
    b. add, add
    c. reduce, complement
    d. add, fortify

60. What are some basic ingredients used to fortify a sauce?
    a. butter
    b. cream
    c. mirepoix, bones
    d. sachet

61. A sauce can have both _____ and _____ flavors.
    a. supporting, distracting
    b. contrasting, complementing
    c. experimental, traditional
    d. none of the above

62. An example of a contemporary sauce is _____
    a. demi glace.
    b. red wine reduction.
    c. red pepper coulis.
    d. all of the above

63. A white sauce should have body and be _____ and reflect the liquid used in preparation.
    a. clear
    b. translucent
    c. shiny
    d. solid

**64.** Generally, hot sauces should be served at what temperature?
   **a.** 150°F
   **b.** 165°F
   **c.** 180°F
   **d.** 212°F

**65.** A sauce is generally *finished* to be customized to the specific dish. What are some methods for finishing sauces?
   **a.** reduction
   **b.** garnish
   **c.** wine
   **d.** all of the above

## Stewing Skills

**66.** Stews are most similar to food that is _____
   **a.** braised.
   **b.** baked.
   **c.** fried.
   **d.** grilled.

**67.** Stews are often _____ dish meals.
   **a.** cold
   **b.** one
   **c.** shallow
   **d.** ceramic

**68.** To make a stew, food is cooked _____
   **a.** quickly.
   **b.** slowly.
   **c.** over high heat.
   **d.** in a microwave.

69. The best pan for a stew is a _____ with _____.
    a. heavy-gauge pan, a lid
    b. lightweight pan, no lid
    c. nonstick pan, no lid
    d. castiron pan, no lid

## Stock-Making Skills

70. Stocks have been described as the _____ of cooking.
    a. foundation
    b. beginning
    c. essence
    d. identity

71. Stocks are made by _____ vegetables, _____, and aromatics in a liquid.
    a. poaching, bones
    b. simmering, fat
    c. simmering, bones
    d. boiling, fat

72. Name three of the five basic stocks.
    a. white, brown, shellfish
    b. beef, veal, chicken
    c. fish, chicken, veal
    d. none of the above

73. A fumet is generally made from the bone of what lean animal?
    a. fish
    b. lamb
    c. young fowl
    d. rabbits

74. When preparing a fumet, the pot should be _____ to retain as much flavor as possible.
    a. strained
    b. covered
    c. deglazed
    d. seasoned

75. A common purpose of stock is to _____
    a. add flavor.
    b. add moisture.
    c. add texture.
    d. all of the above

76. It is not uncommon to find _____ in brown stocks.
    a. tomato paste
    b. wine
    c. brown sugar
    d. none of the above

77. Shellfish stock can be made from _____
    a. lobster shells.
    b. clam shells.
    c. oyster shells.
    d. all of the above

78. Common examples of aromatics are _____
    a. onions.
    b. carrots.
    c. celery.
    d. all of the above

79. A slightly thickened stock is a good substitute for a savory dish that calls for _____
    a. butter.
    b. water.
    c. cream.
    d. none of the above

## Skill-Set 2: Core Competencies

### Knife Skills

80. What are the six parts of a knife?
    a. blade, edge, handle, tamper, point, rivets
    b. edge, honing, tang, point, bolster, rivets
    c. blade, edge, handle, tang, bolster, rivets
    d. blade, tamper, tang, point, bolster, rivets

81. Forged blades are made from _____ metal.
    a. sheet
    b. one piece of
    c. treated
    d. none of the above

82. Metal knives are either _____ or _____.
    a. forged, stamped
    b. steel, aluminum
    c. brass, stainless
    d. pressed, sanded

83. Stamped blades are generally _____ than forged blades.
    a. lighter
    b. less durable
    c. more of a uniform thickness
    d. all of the above

84. A sawtooth knife is generally known as what type of knife?
    a. serrated
    b. tapered
    c. steak
    d. all of the above

85.  A serrated knife is best used for cutting items with a thick _____
     or with a firm _____.
     a.  skin, texture
     b.  crust, skin
     c.  taper, back
     d.  coating, crust

86.  The point at which the handle is attached the knife is known as
     what?
     a.  tang
     b.  drill
     c.  point
     d.  bolster

87.  The tang is actually part of what other piece of the knife?
     a.  blade
     b.  handle
     c.  rivets
     d.  bolster

88.  The bolster acts as the _____ of the knife.
     a.  handle
     b.  collar
     c.  tang
     d.  grip

89.  The rivets hold the _____ together.
     a.  blade
     b.  tang
     c.  handle
     d.  bolster

## Weights and Measures Skills

**90.** 1 liquid tablespoon = _____ teaspoons.
  **a.** 4
  **b.** 2
  **c.** 3
  **d.** 7

**91.** 1 liquid ounce = _____ tablespoons.
  **a.** 3
  **b.** 2
  **c.** 0.5
  **d.** 1.5

**92.** $\frac{3}{8}$ of a cup (liquid) = _____ cup plus _____ tablespoons.
  **a.** $\frac{1}{4}$, 2
  **b.** $\frac{3}{4}$, 1
  **c.** $\frac{1}{4}$, 2.5
  **d.** $\frac{1}{4}$, 3

**93.** Nested measuring cups are best used for _____
  **a.** dry ingredients.
  **b.** liquids.
  **c.** both **a** and **b**
  **d.** none of the above

**94.** T or tbsp is _____
  **a.** the abbreviation for tablespoon.
  **b.** the abbreviation for teaspoon.
  **c.** a type of scale.
  **d.** the equivalent of a pint.

**95.** 1 cup, $\frac{1}{4}$ cup, $\frac{1}{2}$ cup, $\frac{1}{3}$ cup are common sizes of _____

    **a.** spoons.

    **b.** graduated measuring cups.

    **c.** nested measuring cups.

    **d.** all of the above

**96. True or False.** The abbreviation for ounce is *oz.*

**97.** Liquids are best measured in _____

    **a.** nested measuring cups.

    **b.** measuring spoons.

    **c.** graduated measuring cups.

    **d.** small cups.

## Culinary Math Skills

**98.** You are making a triple batch of oatmeal cookies. The original recipe calls for $\frac{3}{4}$ of a teaspoon of salt. How much salt do you need?

    **a.** $1\frac{1}{4}$ tsp

    **b.** $1\frac{1}{2}$ tsp

    **c.** 2 tsp

    **d.** $2\frac{1}{4}$ tsp

**99.** If 147 muffins are needed to feed all of your guests at a brunch you are catering and each muffin pan holds 6 muffins, how many muffin pans do you need to bake them all in one batch?

    **a.** 23

    **b.** 24

    **c.** 25

    **d.** 26

**100.** If each fruit tart is served with 3 fresh strawberries on the plate and 27 people have ordered the fruit tart, how many strawberries do you need total?

    **a.** 9

    **b.** 81

    **c.** 243

    **d.** none of the above

**101.** If you order 80 tuna for your guests and after the meal you have 22 left over, what percentage do you have left?

    **a.** 27.5%

    **b.** 36.3%

    **c.** 58%

    **d.** none of the above

## Skill Set 3: Food Safety and Proper Food Handling

Food-borne illness is a serious concern today. Contamination can come from a number of sources including chemicals in cleaning compounds, insecticides and other toxins, parasites, and bacteria. Many times these contaminations can be avoided through proper food handling and sanitary kitchen procedures. This section will test your knowledge of proper techniques for safety and sanitation in the kitchen.

**102.** Which of the following is one the best defenses against cross-contamination in the kitchen?

    **a.** proper personal hygiene

    **b.** washing hands thoroughly

    **c.** routine sterilization of cooking and food preparation surfaces

    **d.** all of the above

103. When a disease-causing substance is transferred from one contaminated surface this is called _____
    a. cross-contamination.
    b. cooking contamination.
    c. dirty surfaces.
    d. substance transfer.

104. Which of the following should food workers avoid when preparing food?
    a. contagious illness
    b. infected cut on hand
    c. fatigue
    d. all of the above

105. During what time is the greatest risk for contamination in the kitchen?
    a. grilling time
    b. prep time
    c. baking time
    d. the time right after food comes out of the oven

106. **True or False.** Every kitchen needs a fire safety plan.

107. **True or False.** As a general rule, raw food should never touch cooked food.

108. When serving food it is important to use _____ or _____.
    a. utensils, gloves
    b. energy, enthusiasm
    c. bare hands, utensils
    d. none of the above

109. **True or False.** Food should be prepared and served with bare hands.

**110.** Every kitchen needs a _____
    **a.** fire extinguisher.
    **b.** source of water to put out a fire.
    **c.** big lid to cover fires.
    **d.** all of the above

**111. True or False.** Washing your hands thoroughly and properly is one of the best ways to avoid contamination.

## Skill Set 4: Principles of Plating

Proper food presentation is important to making food appealing. While there are no rules as to the right way to plate a meal, this section tests your knowledge of basic standards that add to good plating.

**112.** What is the purpose of a well-thought-out presentation?
    **a.** to enhance the texture of the food
    **b.** to compliment the chef
    **c.** to make the customer want to eat the food
    **d.** to impress the customer

**113.** The main item of a dish should be _____
    **a.** easy to eat.
    **b.** visually appealing.
    **c.** surrounded by complementary or contrasting flavors.
    **d.** all of the above

**114.** What sense does a well-organized plate takes advantage of?
    **a.** sight
    **b.** sound
    **c.** smell
    **d.** all of the above

115. What might you expect to see in a well-organized plating presentation?
    a. main food item
    b. garnish
    c. side dish
    d. all of the above

116. What should draw your attention to a well-dressed plate?
    a. garnish
    b. side
    c. focal point
    d. none of the above

117. The _____ is the canvas for your presentation.
    a. sauce
    b. plate
    c. main item
    d. garnish

118. Who is responsible for maintaining sanitized serving dishes for service?
    a. sous chef
    b. head chef
    c. kitchen manager
    d. dishwasher

119. A _____ presentation has equal numbers and shapes on both sides of a main item.
    a. symmetrical
    b. asymmetrical
    c. contrasting
    d. complementary

120. A (n) _____ presentation has unequal numbers and shapes on both sides of a main item.
    a. symmetrical
    b. asymmetrical
    c. contrasting
    d. complementary

121. Cold foods should be served on _____ dishes.
    a. room temperature
    b. cold
    c. warm
    d. all of the above

## Skill Set 5: Organization of a Professional Kitchen

A properly organized kitchen is one of the keys to a successful food operation. This section tests your knowledge on the stations in the kitchen and the various jobs that make up the kitchen career ladder.

122. What station must your first master before becoming a head chef?
    a. all stations
    b. sous station
    c. fry station
    d. salad station

123. What person is widely regarded as the second in command in the professional kitchen?
    a. fry chef
    b. sous chef
    c. commis
    d. expediter

**124.** Who is the person responsible for accepting orders into the kitchen and relaying them to the various stations?
- **a.** waiter
- **b.** sous chef
- **c.** expediter
- **d.** manager

**125.** Generally speaking, who is the last person to see a dish before it is served?
- **a.** head chef
- **b.** sous chef
- **c.** expediter
- **d.** manager

**126.** Who is the person responsible for all fried foods?
- **a.** grill chef
- **b.** fry chef
- **c.** head chef
- **d.** commis

**127.** Where is a swing cook's main station?
- **a.** fried foods station
- **b.** appetizers station
- **c.** wherever needed
- **d.** grilled foods station

**128.** The cold food station chef is known as a _____
- **a.** garde manger.
- **b.** commis.
- **c.** sous chef.
- **d.** chef de cuisine.

**129.** A head chef is also known as _____
   a. executive chef.
   b. chef de cuisine.
   c. sous chef.
   d. a and b only.

**130.** What responsibilities might a garde manger have?
   a. salads
   b. appetizers
   c. prep cook
   d. all of the above

**131.** What is the name for the type of kitchen system that has multiple stations?
   a. brigade system
   b. station system
   c. stepped system
   d. none of the above

**132.** What is the common name for someone who works on all stations but is not the head chef?
   a. line cook
   b. prep cook
   c. brigade cook
   d. brigadier

## PRACTICE TEST 2

### Skill Set 1: Basic Culinary Concepts and Methods

**Baking Skills**

1. What kind of heat is used for baking?
   a. moist
   b. direct
   c. dry
   d. high

2. Beurage dough has what as a main ingredient?
   a. butter
   b. sugar
   c. molasses
   d. honey

3. Prebaking an empty crust is known as what?
   a. blind baking
   b. docking
   c. pinning
   d. proofing

4. **True or False.** Baking powder and baking soda are used as leavening agents.

5. A pâte à choux consists of water, butter, _____, and _____.
   a. flour, yeast
   b. flour, milk
   c. yeast, eggs
   d. flour, eggs

6. A (n) _____ uses a pâte à choux.
   a. pancake
   b. cookie
   c. éclair
   d. puff pastry

7. **True or False.** The main difference between custard and pastry cream is flour.

8. Pancake batter is an example of the _____ method.
   a. creaming
   b. well mixing
   c. sifting
   d. docking

9. Custards require _____, egg, and _____.
   a. cream or milk, sugar
   b. water, sugar
   c. melted butter, sugar
   d. cream or milk, salt

10. When making custards, it is best to _____ the eggs with the hot liquids to avoid scrambling the eggs.
    a. temper
    b. cream
    c. mix
    d. pour

## Braising Skills

11. _____ is a method of thickening the braising liquid.
    a. Natural reduction
    b. Adding a slurry
    c. Dredging the meat in flout before searing
    d. all of the above

12. _____ is a common braised dish.
    a. Chicken noodle soup
    b. Pot roast
    c. Barbeque ribs
    d. Brisket

13. White stews of small game animals such as rabbit are called
    _____
    a. fricassee.
    b. blanquette.
    c. bouillabaisse.
    d. goulash.

14. _____ is generally known as a Hungarian beef, veal, poultry, or
    pork stew colored and flavored with paprika.
    a. Fricassee
    b. Blanquette
    c. Bouillabaisse
    d. Goulash

15. White braised foods that are finished with mushrooms and pearl
    onions are called _____
    a. fricassee.
    b. blanquette.
    c. bouillabaisse.
    d. goulash.

16. **True or False.** A roux can be used to thicken a braising liquid.

17. **True or False.** Braising is an appropriate cooking method for
    cooking chicken breast.

18. **True or False.** In the braising cooking method, moist heat is
    used.

19. **True or False.** Braised items should shred and fall apart when cooked properly.

20. **True or False.** Braised items have a deep, rich sauce.

21. **True or False.** Vegetables and other aromatics such as garlic should not be used for braising.

## Grilling Skills

22. Mesquite, apple, peach, and hickory are _____
    a. types of fruits.
    b. types of wood used to add flavor to grilled foods.
    c. names of grills.
    d. salt rubs.

23. Planks and chips are _____
    a. wood products that add flavor to grilled foods.
    b. utensils for grilling.
    c. ways to prepare food for grilling.
    d. grilling processes.

24. **True or False.** Grilling food makes it tender.

25. Meat or poultry should be cut into _____ for best grilled results.
    a. portion sizes
    b. small chunks
    c. large flat pieces
    d. thick slices

26. _____ is the proper lubricant for grill rods.
    a. Salt
    b. Herbs
    c. Vinegar
    d. Oil

27. **True or False.** Generally, food should be seasoned before it is grilled.

28. You should remove food from the grill when it _____
    a. is dark and charred.
    b. has grill marks on both sides.
    c. is slightly underdone.
    d. appears dry.

29. The smoky flavor that comes from grilling should _____
    a. overpower food's taste.
    b. enhance food's taste
    c. be added after food is cooked.
    d. make food last longer.

30. Keeping a grill _____ will enhance food's flavor.
    a. full of charcoal
    b. cold before cooking
    c. clean and well oiled
    d. covered

31. Which of the following items can be used in grilling?
    a. baskets, skewers, and racks
    b. wood chips, marinades, and salt rubs
    c. tongs, herbs, and oil
    d. all of the above

## Pastry Skills

32. **True or False.** Making sure all dry ingredients are blended well will cut down on mixing time later.

33. Overmixing a pastry batter can result in _____
    a. producing too much gluten.
    b. making batter lumpy.
    c. the batter burning when baked.
    d. none of the above

34. Pastry dough is best when the dough is _____
    a. made with oil.
    b. worked with when it is warm.
    c. worked as little as possible.
    d. all of the above

35. Butter, lard, and shortening are the most common fats used for
    the _____ method.
    a. rubbed dough
    b. cutting in
    c. chopping in
    d. a and b only

36. The cutting method produces _____ and _____ doughs.
    a. flaky, mealy
    b. flaky, crusty
    c. smooth, sugary
    d. none of the above

37. Flaky pie dough is best used for _____
    a. pastries with cream filling.
    b. pies with fruit filling.
    c. tarts with chocolate filling.
    d. all of the above

38. An oven for making pastry should be _____
    a. preheated.
    b. cold.
    c. very hot.
    d. none of the above

39. Which of the following best describes the blending method for making pastry dough?
    a. combining dry and wet ingredients in separate bowls, and then mixing them together
    b. rubbing chilled butter into dry ingredients
    c. putting all ingredients in one bowl and mixing with a mixer
    d. adding ingredients to the bowl as they appear in the recipe

40. What type of fat is used with the blending method?
    a. cold solid butter
    b. chilled lard
    c. oil or melted butter
    d. none of the above

41. When using the blending method, fat should be added to the bowl with the _____
    a. dry ingredients.
    b. wet ingredients.
    c. eggs.
    d. all of the above

## Poaching Skills

42. Which best describe shallow poaching?
    a. completely submerging an item in a liquid kept at a constant moderate temperature
    b. partially submerging an item in a liquid kept at a constant high temperature
    c. completely submerging an item in a liquid kept at a constant high temperature
    d. partially submerging an item in a liquid kept at a constant moderate temperature

43. The aim of poaching is to produce foods that are _____ and
    tender.
    a. well done
    b. moist
    c. bite sized
    d. hot

44. What is the appropriate temperature for the poaching liquid?
    a. 160°F to 185°F
    b. 185°F to 212°F
    c. 155°F to 170°F
    d. 145°F to 160°F

45. Which of the following is an appropriate cooking liquid for
    poaching?
    a. water
    b. stock
    c. wine
    d. all of the above

## Roasting Skills

To answer question 46, choose the correct definition of the underlined
word.

46. After roasting, save the pan <u>drippings</u> to make gravy.
    a. fat
    b. fond
    c. skin
    d. all of the above

47. Roasting is best in a _____ oven.
    a. cold
    b. preheated
    c. low-temperature
    d. none of the above

48. Basting with butter, oil, or marinade adds _____ to food.
    a. flavor
    b. moisture
    c. both **a** and **b**
    d. none of the above

49. _____ food prior to roasting to reduce the fat.
    a. Trim
    b. Cut
    c. Salt
    d. Weigh

## Sauce-Making Skills

50. A sauce should have which of the following flavors?
    a. bold
    b. natural
    c. balanced
    d. none of the above

51. Methods of thickening a sauce include which of the following?
    a. adding a roux
    b. adding a slurry
    c. natural reduction
    d. all of the above

52. *Slurry* is defined as an uncooked paste of a cold liquid such as _____ and a nonprotein starch such as _____.
    a. alcohol, cornstarch
    b. beer, rice flour
    c. water, potato starch
    d. all of the above

53. A slurry is usually added to a _____ liquid.
    a. cold
    b. hot
    c. room temperature
    d. all of the above

54. A *roux* is defined as a cooked paste of _____ and _____.
    a. flour, fat
    b. oil, butter
    c. water, flour
    d. milk, flour

55. When adding liquid to a roux, _____ to avoid lumping.
    a. stir occasionally
    b. add salt
    c. whisk constantly
    d. temper butter

56. Classic white sauces like velouté and béchamel are produced by adding what as a thickener?
    a. a roux
    b. a slurry
    c. cream
    d. cornstarch

57. _____ and _____ are the most typical flavors that finish a tomato sauce.
    a. Oregano, basil
    b. Garlic, salt
    c. Onion, garlic
    d. Thyme, rosemary

58. Some tomatoes have a high _____ content.
    a. acid
    b. fat
    c. salt
    d. water

59. When making a sauce, it is important to heat the pot evenly to avoid _____
    a. boiling.
    b. burning.
    c. scorching.
    d. ruining.

## Sauté Skills

60. _____ foods are best sautéed.
    a. Thick
    b. Tender
    c. Salted
    d. Sweetened

61. If food tastes dry after sautéing, it usually means the food was
    _____
    a. not fresh.
    b. overcooked.
    c. undercooked.
    d. too spicy.

62. **True or False.** Sautéing is an excellent method for cooking vegetables.

63. Sautéing vegetables is most like _____
    a. glazing.
    b. stir frying.
    c. stewing.
    d. simmering.

64. _____ is a technique used to reheat fully cooked or to complete cooking partially sautéed vegetables.
    a. Finishing
    b. Glazing
    c. Poaching
    d. none of the above

65. Using too much fat when sautéing can lead to food _____
    a. drying out.
    b. frying.
    c. tasting salty.
    d. none of the above

66. Using oil that is not hot enough can cause sautéed food to _____
    a. burn.
    b. brown.
    c. absorb oil.
    d. crumble.

67. **True or False.** Sautéing wet food can cause food to stew.

68. _____ is a method used when sautéing food.
    a. Tossing
    b. Shaking
    c. Turning
    d. all of the above

## Stewing Skills

69. Which of the following makes stewing different from braising?
    a. stewing uses larger pieces of food
    b. stewing uses smaller pieces of food
    c. food is cooked at hotter temperatures
    d. food sits overnight

70. **True or False.** The stewing method of cooking food takes less time than braising.

71. Which of the following can be used to thicken a stew?
    a. roux
    b. fat
    c. sugar
    d. salt

## Stock-Making Skills

72. Equipment for preparing stocks may include _____ and _____.
    a. stockpot, skimmer
    b. stockpot, thermometer
    c. thermometer, whisk
    d. all of the above

73. To make a clean and clear stock, it is best to _____ when cooking.
    a. skim the fat
    b. strain the stock
    c. stir the stock
    d. none of the above

74. To make a clean and clear stock, it is also best to _____ when cooking.
    a. boil rapidly
    b. disrupt bones and vegetable as much as possible
    c. simmer slowly
    d. brown all bones

75. Which of the following would produce a cloudy stock?
    a. boiling
    b. stirring
    c. covering the pot
    d. all of the above

76. Since vegetable and bones are usually removed from stock once cooked, it is not necessary to _____ the vegetables.
    a. clean
    b. peel
    c. chop
    d. all of the above

77. When preparing brown stock, doing what to the bones will add additional flavor?
    a. roasting
    b. poaching
    c. braising
    d. boiling

78. Another common method to add additional flavor to a brown stock is to add a _____ onion.
    a. burnt
    b. cooked
    c. boiled
    d. none of the above

79. _____ are not an appropriate vegetable for stock making.
    a. Tomatoes
    b. Potatoes
    c. Carrots
    d. Parsnips

80. Generally, _____ is/are not added when preparing stocks.
    a. salt
    b. pepper
    c. herbs
    d. spices

81. As a general rule of thumb, a chicken stock should simmer for
_____ hour(s).
    a. 1
    b. 3
    c. 6
    d. 4

## Skill Set 2: Core Competencies

### Knife Skills

82. When first learning how to handle a knife, _____ is the main
objective.
    a. speed
    b. accuracy
    c. maneuvering
    d. cleanliness

83. Knife blades are given an edge on a _____ stone.
    a. sharpening
    b. honing
    c. grooming
    d. filing

84. Knives are maintained mostly by _____.
    a. sharpening
    b. cleaning
    c. grooming
    d. filing

85. Knife safety dictates that you never attempt to _____ a falling
knife.
    a. catch
    b. stop
    c. grasp
    d. all of the above

86. Before storing a knife, it always a good idea to _____ it.
    a. sharpen
    b. sanitize
    c. hone
    d. all of the above

87. When sharpening a blade, it important to pass the blade _____
    a. at a 40° angle.
    b. in the same direction each time.
    c. perpendicularly.
    d. from point to heel.

88. Always hold a knife by its _____
    a. handle.
    b. tang.
    c. bolster.
    d. rivets.

89. When sharpening a knife, one should hold the knife at a _____ angle.
    a. 10°–15°
    b. 15°–20°
    c. 20°–25°
    d. 40°–45°

90. What is the hand NOT holding the knife called?
    a. the guiding hand
    b. the left hand
    c. the right hand
    d. the straight hand

91. Basic cuts include which of the following?
    a. chopping, mincing
    b. dice, rondelle
    c. batonnet, julienne
    d. all of the above

92. What is the purpose of evenly cut items?
    a. show precision
    b. even cooking
    c. add flavor
    d. none of the above

## Weights and Measures Skills

93. **True or False.** Measuring spoons can be used for dry and liquid ingredients.

94. 4 tablespoons = _____ cup = _____ ounces
    a. $\frac{1}{3}$, 4
    b. $\frac{1}{2}$, 2
    c. $\frac{1}{4}$, 2
    d. $\frac{1}{8}$, 2

95. 1 cup = _____ fluid ounces
    a. 10
    b. 16
    c. 4
    d. 8

96. There are _____ cups in a pint.
    a. 1
    b. 2
    c. 3
    d. 4

97. **True or False.** 12 Tablespoons = 1 cup.

98. A bushel is equivalent to 4 _____.
    a. pecks
    b. quarts
    c. kilograms
    d. cups

**99.** How many fluid ounces make up 1 gallon?

    **a.** 64

    **b.** 36

    **c.** 72

    **d.** 128

**100.** _____ tablespoons = 3 teaspoons

    **a.** 1

    **b.** 2

    **c.** 3

    **d.** 4

**101.** 1 gallon = _____ quarts

    **a.** 16

    **b.** 4

    **c.** 8

    **d.** 32

## Culinary Math Skills

**102.** If Barry orders 400 cupcakes, but the bakery fails to deliver 16% of his order, how many cupcakes are missing?

    **a.** 316

    **b.** 226

    **c.** 336

    **d.** 64

**103.** The salaries for the staff at Ms. Halpern's restaurant total $8,000 per month. Her annual sales amount to $1,400,000. Approximately what percentage of her annual sales do salaries represent?

    **a.** 6.5%

    **b.** 6.8%

    **c.** 6.9%

    **d.** 7.0%

**104.** Mr. Posnick bought $110 worth of sugar from Mr. Annunziata. Because Mr. Posnick is such a loyal customer, Mr. Annunziata only charged Mr. Posnick $94.60. What percentage discount did Mr. Posnick get?

   **a.** 6%

   **b.** 11%

   **c.** 14%

   **d.** none of the above

**105.** If you have 4 pies, and 22 people who want a slice of pie, into how many equal pieces should you cut each pie so that everyone gets a slice and has the largest possible slice of pie?

   **a.** 5

   **b.** 6

   **c.** 7

   **d.** 8

**106.** If you are baking a half batch of banana bread and the original recipe calls for $1\frac{1}{2}$ cups of walnuts, how many walnuts do you need?

   **a.** $\frac{1}{2}$ cup

   **b.** $\frac{1}{4}$ cup

   **c.** $\frac{3}{4}$ cup

   **d.** none of the above

## Skill Set 3: Food Safety and Proper Food Handling

**107.** _____ can help make sure food that you use is not contaminated.

   **a.** Close inspection

   **b.** Ordering from vendors you know and trust

   **c.** Proper storage

   **d.** all of the above

108. Iodine, chlorine, and quaternary ammonium are all _____
    a. cleaning compounds.
    b. sanitizing compounds.
    c. used to clear away dirt and dust.
    d. used for cooking.

109. All remodeling and construction in a restaurant must meet _____ standards.
    a. ADA
    b. OSHA
    c. DEA
    d. USDA

110. Which of the following is NOT the purpose of the chef's hat?
    a. to provide a fashion accessory
    b. to keep hair from falling in the food
    c. to keep sweat off the brow
    d. all of the above

111. _____ may be contained in raw egg yolks.
    a. Salmonella
    b. Citronella
    c. Bicarbonate
    d. Bird flu

112. The proper temperature to store cold food is _____.
    a. 40°F or below until serving.
    b. 30°F or below until serving.
    c. 25°F or below until serving.
    d. 50°F or below until serving.

113. **True or False.** Hot food should be kept at 140°F or above until serving.

**114.** Which of the following foods is NOT on the FDA's food allergen list?

   **a.** eggs

   **b.** shellfish

   **c.** broccoli

   **d.** peanuts

**115.** Dry storage is NOT recommended for what types of foods?

   **a.** sugar

   **b.** dairy

   **c.** canned goods

   **d.** flour

**116.** One of the leading causes of food-borne illness is _____

   **a.** improper cooling and storage of food.

   **b.** adding too much sugar to food.

   **c.** adding too much salt to food.

   **d.** overcooking food.

## Skill Set 4: Principles of Plating

**117.** Hot foods should be served on _____ dishes.

   **a.** room temp

   **b.** cold

   **c.** warm

   **d.** all of the above

**118.** Generally speaking, adding _____ adds drama to a plate.

   **a.** greens

   **b.** flavor

   **c.** height

   **d.** texture

119. What may be a good idea for items that do not have a shape on their own, such as rice pilaf?
    a. place into a mold before serving
    b. serve on the side
    c. make into a main dish
    d. all of the above

120. What is a nonfunctional garnish?
    a. an edible garnish
    b. an inedible garnish
    c. a garnish that adds only color
    d. a presentation dressing

121. A garnish that adds an extra dimension to the dish beyond color is known as?
    a. a functional garnish
    b. an edible garnish
    c. an inedible garnish
    d. a presentation dressing

122. Garnishes should be _____
    a. edible.
    b. chopped.
    c. of like flavor.
    d. none of the above

## Skill Set 5: Organization of a Professional Kitchen

123. In modern kitchens the multiple-station system is known as _____
    a. the prep area.
    b. the line.
    c. the kitchen.
    d. none of the above

124. Preparation work for service is formally known as _____
   a. prep.
   b. mise en place.
   c. journaling.
   d. bridging.

125. What might the responsibilities of a pastry chef include?
   a. dinner service
   b. preparing all baked goods
   c. serving desserts
   d. all of the above

126. In a professional kitchen, _____ is paramount.
   a. speed
   b. cleanliness
   c. the ability to work on your own
   d. all of the above

127. A person responsible for preparation work may be known as a
   _____
   a. line cook.
   b. prep cook.
   c. brigade cook.
   d. brigadier.

128. Which of the following ranks highest in a professional kitchen?
   a. sous chef
   b. chef de cuisine
   c. commis
   d. fry chef

129. Which of the following ranks lowest in a professional kitchen?
   a. sous chef
   b. chef de cuisine
   c. commis
   d. chef de partie

**130.** An apprentice is known as a _____
    **a.** sous chef.
    **b.** chef de cuisine.
    **c.** commis.
    **d.** fry chef.

**131.** Kitchen design is important in what aspect of the restaurant?
    **a.** cleanliness
    **b.** efficiency
    **c.** speed
    **d.** menu design

**132.** A kitchen that has a large stove for boiling water may specialize in _____ cuisine.
    **a.** Middle Eastern
    **b.** Scandinavian
    **c.** French
    **d.** Spanish

# CHAPTER five

## HOW TO LAND A GREAT CULINARY JOB

**APPROACH YOUR** job search with focus, determination, and a positive attitude, and you will be sure to come out a winner. Many tools exist to help you land a great job in the culinary arts. Before you start gearing up for the job hunt, however, take some time to evaluate your interests, desires, and personal financial situation. Culinary educator and chef Geraldine Born gives this advice to her culinary students before they go out to look for a job. She says:

> *Take a long look at yourself to understand what makes you happy. Do you enjoy following recipes? Would you mind doing that every day? If not, then perhaps working in a franchise restaurant is for you. However, if you prefer something more creative, then you'll want to go*

*where you'll have the chance to come up with new recipes—perhaps an independent restaurant that offers dinner specials or a mom and pop place that allows flexibility in menu planning. Or if you love garde manger, then look for a job with a banquet hall or a hotel that regularly hosts banquets. If you desire a good benefits package and moderate hours, you may look at jobs in institutional cooking. You need to know yourself and where your interests lie, so you can choose the position that is best for you.*

—Geraldine Born, Culinary Educator

Once you have focused in on an area of culinary arts that appeals to you, how do you go about getting a great job in that area? Read on to learn about the latest job hunting tools you can use to secure a culinary position that's right for you.

## CONDUCTING YOUR JOB SEARCH

Using several different methods of job searching will increase your chances for success. For instance, do not rely exclusively on a single online job search engine to conduct your search. If you take advantage of all the job hunting resources that are available today, you can locate and apply for jobs all over the country. One excellent resource you can use if you are in a culinary training program is the school's job placement office.

### The Internet

The first place you will likely start your job search is the Internet. If you do not have your own computer, try to access one at your local public library, or at school if you are attending classes. Many professional associations host websites that include industry information and some also include job-related information. The federal government and several national private job banks also have websites with thousands of job listings all over the country. You can of course search the all-encompassing job search sites such as Monster.com, Indeed.com, Careerbuider.com, Hotjobs.com and

Linkedin.com. For more direct targeting, here is a list of several online re-sources that post information specifically about culinary arts jobs.

### www.careersinfood.com

With over 5,000 current food and beverage manufacturing jobs posted from hundreds of the industry's top companies and recruiters, this site claims to be the largest food and beverage industry–specific job board on the Internet.

### www.starchefsjobfinder.com

This site allows you to search for industry positions from entry-level line cooks to senior FOH (front-of-house) management: restaurant jobs, cook jobs, chef jobs, hotel jobs, and all foodservice employment.

### www.chef2chef.net/

The Chef2Chef job board posts restaurant and foodservice employment positions including executive chef, sous chef, cook, waiter, bartender, and culinary instructor positions.

### www.escoffier.com

This site, called Escoffier On Line (EOL), offers information about foodservice employment and education. The site includes searchable *Help Wanted* and *Position Sought* sections.

### www.hospitalitylink.com

This website, Hospitality Link, is focused on employment and staffing for the hospitality industry. You can click on *Culinary* to access nationwide job openings for chefs, pastry chefs, executive chefs, and sous chefs. The site also offers links to recruiters, employers, resume services, industry-related sites, and resume postings.

### www.coolworks.com

Coolworks provides links to job openings at camps, resorts, cruise ships, guest ranches, and more. Many of the jobs are in the hospitality and foodservice industry; some are seasonal and some are permanent. The job openings are organized by state or by job category, such as camp jobs, resort jobs, cruise ship jobs, and so on.

**www.usajobs.opm.gov**

If you are looking for a cooking job with the federal government, check out this website of the United States Office of Personnel Management.

**www.nacufs.org**

This is the site for the National Association of College & University Food Services (NACUFS), a trade association for foodservice professionals at hundreds of institutions of higher education in the United States, Canada, and abroad. It includes a job bulletin with many open managerial positions at NACUFS schools such as chef, sous chef, executive chef, banquet manager, foodservice manager, catering manager, director, and more.

## Your School's Job Placement Office

If you are attending a culinary school, or if you have graduated from one that offers job placement assistance for alumni, this will be an invaluable tool for your job hunt. Many culinary schools provide a wide range of services to aid students in their job search. Visit the job placement office, ask some questions, and find out what your school's job placement rate of success is. It may calm your fears of landing a good job upon graduation. Some schools claim that 90%–100% of their graduates obtain jobs within six months of graduation. Other schools boast that their graduates get four or five different job offers to choose from. Ask about which services the job placement office offers to students. You may be able to obtain personalized career counseling, participate in mock interviews, or attend a campus job fair. Ask a counselor in the placement office for a list of the alumni who are willing to network with students for job leads. Take advantage of as many services as you possibly can to increase your odds of landing your dream job.

## Your Public Library

Visit your local public library; it has a wealth of information available about the culinary arts industry and tools to help in your job search. For example, many libraries carry periodicals that focus on the industry, such as *Bon Appétit*, *Gourmet*, or *Food and Wine*. You may want to browse through these magazines to locate restaurants or chefs you are interested in. Then ask a librarian how to find the phone number, website, or address of a particular restaurant discussed in one of the magazines—and you will have a possible job lead. E-mail or call the chef at the restaurant to inquire about possible job openings.

You can also ask a reference librarian where the library's *Career* section is located, so you can browse through books on job hunting and writing resumes. Be sure to look in both the circulating and reference collections.

Finally, many libraries have online tools, often containing job listings and practice tests, to help in your career search. One such tool is LearningExpress Library. This innovative web solution, available in over 4,000 public libraries, includes test-preparation tools, skill-building materials, and career resources. Additionally, it features over 770 online practice tests and interactive skill-building tutorials, along with more than 130 e-book titles developed by expert academic and industry professionals. For more information on LearningExpress Library, visit your local library or see the website at www.learningexpressllc.com/library.

## SAMPLE JOB POSTINGS

The following sample job postings will give you an idea of what type of requirements and pay levels are available. Keep in mind that job duties, benefits, and salaries vary considerably, but these postings culled from a variety of sources can give you an idea of what is available.

| | |
|---|---|
| Position: | Sous Chef |
| Location: | Long Beach, California |
| Requirements: | Must be innovative and creative. One year's experience in similar position as sous chef. Must be ready to apply yourself. Culinary degree preferred. |
| Description: | New 100-seat upscale restaurant needs sous chef to create something special. Open for lunch and dinner, seven days a week. Two weeks paid vacation. Chance to work with a successful chef. |
| Salary: | $30,000–34,000 annually |

| | |
|---|---|
| Position: | Pastry Chef |
| Location: | Vail, Colorado |
| Description: | Create and prepare all items for dessert menu. Prepare and display creative desserts for banquets, create birthday cakes, cookies, pies etc. for a four-diamond property. |
| Requirements: | Knowledge of bake shop techniques required. Minimum of five year's pastry experience and culinary training preferred. Creativity and willingness to work flexible schedule is required. |
| Salary: | $11–$16 per hour, depending on experience. Excellent benefits package included. |

## THE JOBS ARE OUT THERE

The service industry is one of the fastest growing in the United States. According to the Bureau of Labor Statistics, by 2018, service-providing industries are expected to account for 131 million out of 154 million wage and salary jobs overall.

—*Bureau of Labor Statistics*

## MARKETING YOURSELF

Although you may not think about the need to promote yourself, recognition can be critical for your career success in the competitive culinary industry. The following strategies will help you to promote your career.

### Networking

Networking is major job search tactic used by people in all industries. Essentially, it is just talking to people you already know or meeting new people to talk about some aspect of the culinary arts. For instance, you can network with your friends, relatives, and acquaintances to find out if they know of a restaurant that is hiring or of an experienced chef in your area who would be an excellent mentor. And you can network with other cooks and chefs to find out whether they like where they work. Once you land a job, you will probably be networking with your coworkers to find out more information about various specialties in the culinary arts field, such as pastry arts, garde manger, meat cutting, and others.

You can add to your network when you visit various kitchens looking for employment. While most cooks and chefs are very busy, they often will take a few minutes out of their day to talk to a newcomer in the field. They were beginners once themselves, so if you are careful not to take up too much of their time, they may give you some useful information. Here are some typical questions you can ask cooks about their jobs:

▶ How do you like working here?
▶ What are the benefits of working here?
▶ What is the kitchen atmosphere like?
▶ How does the executive chef treat you?
▶ Where else have you worked, and how does this place compare?

You can gather a lot of information in a casual way, just by talking to as many people as you can. When you leave each kitchen or restaurant, jot down some notes on what you heard and learned, so you can organize the information and access it later. After you have talked to a lot of people in different kitchens, it is easy to forget what each person had to say.

Networking with other culinary arts professionals can also give you inside information on local or regional trends. You can find out what other chefs are doing and which restaurants are hiring. You may also get the scoop on which chefs are planning to expand their kitchens to include pastry chefs or additional workers. Then you can add those kitchens to your list of places to visit.

### Maintaining Your Contacts

It is important to maintain your contacts once you have established them. Try to contact people again within a couple of weeks of meeting them. You can always ask a question, convey a piece of information related to your conversation, or just send a note of thanks. This contact will cement your meeting in their minds, so they will remember you more readily when you get in touch in the future. If you have not communicated with your contacts for a few months, you might send them a note or e-mail about an article you read, a special culinary technique, or relevant new culinary tool, just to keep your name fresh in their minds.

### Contacting Chefs

After narrowing your list down to three or four chefs for whom you would like to work, the next step is to gain an interview. You should find out the schedule of each chef before trying to make contact. Once you have determined a convenient time, call the chefs and tell them that you are interested in working for them. Ask if there are currently any openings and if so, request an interview. Even if there are no openings in their kitchen, ask whether you can come in to observe or work in the kitchen for a few days for free. That way, you can gather more information, make a good impression, and find out whether you can apply after gaining more experience. Bring a few copies of your resume with you when you visit each chef's kitchen.

### Business Cards

Another way to promote yourself is with business cards that list your name, contact information, and any certifications you have earned. Carry them with you at all times and hand them out every chance you get. Keep the cards simple and professional. You can print them on your own computer, purchase them at an office supply store, or order them online at websites such as www.vistaprint.com.

## Websites, Blogs, and Online Social Networking

Using online tools can be one of the most effective ways to market yourself. Taking the time to create a personal webpage that highlights your culinary skills, resume, and accomplishments is a great way to distinguish yourself in this industry. You may want to post pictures of your favorite dishes so people get a sense of your cooking style. If the site is well done, you can reference your website in your cover letter when applying to jobs.

Many people hire a professional to design their websites. If you prefer to do it yourself, you will need to choose an available domain name, find a web host, and then either design it yourself if you know HTML or another programming language, or use a website builder. To find a website builder, just type *how to create an easy website* as a Google search and you will find several options.

A *blog* (short for *weblog*) is an online journal in which people can publish their thoughts and opinions as many times a day as they please. Blogging can also be a great way to market yourself and connect with others with similar interests. If you post to a blog daily about your profession and also comment regularly on other professionals' blogs in the industry, eventually you could get a following. Popularity can lead to name recognition in the industry, which could open the door for you toward new job opportunities. If you do not post solely about yourself, you may want to consider starting a blog on a culinary-related topic that is of particular interest to you. Just as regular websites, there are many providers available to host your blog. The most popular are www.blogger.com, www.xanga.com, www.wordpress.com, and www.livejournal.com. Most providers are free and easy to use.

There are many social networking sites available today. You probably already have either a Facebook® or a MySpace® account. If you are creative, you can use these tools to create a thorough online profile that will help promote your culinary interests and skills. One note of caution: if you are using these types of tools for professional networking, you may want to avoid posting personal information such as pictures from your last vacation or your favorite jokes, as this may leave a bad impression on a potential employer. Finally, some social networking sites, such as www.linkedin.com, are more professional in nature. LinkedIn is a great way to network with other culinary professionals, list your resume, learn more about the industry, and even find out about current job openings.

## Volunteering

Volunteering your time at restaurants, hotels, or other establishments can have numerous benefits. First, you will gain valuable experience by observing how the kitchen functions and watching the chefs themselves. Additionally, it is a chance to network with others and to market yourself as a potential candidate when a position becomes available at that location. Finally, by volunteering several times, you can start to gain a reputation as someone who is committed to learning more about the industry and furthering your career.

In most cities, restaurant managers and chefs will talk among each other frequently. You want them to be saying positive things about you. Remember, word of mouth can be a powerful marketing tool.

## RESUME BASICS

As you make your career path, the one constant that will follow you wherever you go is your resume. It is important to understand nuances for the food industry that will help make your resume the best showcase for your work and talents. Make your resume stand out and say something unique about you. Include information that sets you apart from other candidates. Do you have any special skills, such as knowledge of one or more foreign languages? Did you help create any dishes that are now part of the regular menu where you used to work? Do you do any charitable volunteer work using your culinary skills? All of this information can be incorporated into your resume to pique the interest of potential employers.

Here are some overall rules to adhere to when writing your resume:

1. **Organization.** No matter what job in any industry you are applying for, it is essential to have a neat, clean, and organized resume. Remember, the resume is often the first impression you give to an employer. Long before you have the opportunity to meet face to face, your resume speaks for you. No misspellings or inaccuracies are acceptable. Such errors show that you did not take the time to make sure your resume was perfect, and can make the potential employer wonder whether you would take the time to make sure a sauce or dressing was seasoned perfectly. Double and triple check your spelling.

2. **Quickly readable.** Use bullets for your entries to keep them brief and to the point. While it is understandable that you are trying to include as much information about yourself as possible, remember that when employers feel they are wading through an overwritten resume, they may easily give up and move on to a cleaner, more focused resume.

3. **Short.** Try to keep your resume to one page; two at a maximum if you have many years of experience. Again, remember you are trying to communicate the most information in the smallest amount of space.

4. **Language.** Use action words, such as *managed*, *conducted*, *developed*, or *produced*. This helps emphasize your accomplishments.

5. **Easily readable.** Use a legible, attractive font and choose good quality paper when you print out copies. These small touches will make a big difference in how you come off to employers.

6. **Do not include** personal information such as your birth date, race, marital status, or religion.

Let us take a look at some of the essential parts of a culinary resume and consider how to use them to present yourself in the best possible way.

1. **Name.** The top of your resume should include your name, contact information, and e-mail address. Emphasize your name either by making it larger than anything else on the page or by making it **bold** or *italic*, or some combination thereof. Be sure that your e-mail address is professional. Cute e-mail addresses are fine for friends and family, but they are not appropriate on a resume. Some job seekers also include an objective (the type of job they are looking for) right after their name, but this is optional.

2. **Education.** Focus on your culinary education. Hiring chefs are often very interested in where you went to school. Once you gain some experience, it is possible to list your work experience above your education. While it is not imperative for every restaurant worker to go to culinary school in order to perform well, the truth is that, with increased competition, a chef might be more likely to hire you and consider you for advancement if your background includes a diploma from a respected school. List the names of all schools you have attended, including high school and college, with complete address, telephone, and e-mail information. If you graduated with any honors or won any special awards be sure to mention that fact. Keep all your culinary education listed together and make it clearly readable at the top of your resume.

3. **Work experience.** After your education, list any work experience you want considered. This can include your work on an internship or as an apprentice. Take your time to ensure that the details you include in this section properly reflect and highlight your duties at each job. If you are a career changer, be careful only to include work that is relevant to what you are looking to do now. Make sure your job descriptions reflect clearly why each job outside the culinary field prepared you for a unique contribution that you intend to make in your new culinary life and developed a skill you possess that amplifies your culinary skills.

   Include the names of all chefs under whom you worked, along with complete address information for each restaurant or establishment. Clearly list the dates you worked, including month and year. Never lie. If you have room, it is also helpful to include some detail about the places you have worked, including the size of the restaurant, the number of seats, and the volume of business, particularly if you are applying for a job in a new city or another part of the country. Make sure to describe the kinds of dishes and cuisines you worked with and to note any information on promotions you received.

4. **References.** Employers interested in hiring you may want speak to people who can accurately describe your work experience and personal qualities—that is, your references. How do you come up with references? The first step is to create a list of former supervisors, chef-instructors, or other professionals with whom you have interacted. You want to select people who know you well and who would heartily recommend you to an employer. (Be aware that it is standard practice *not* to include relatives as references.) Before you narrow down your list to three or four people, contact each person to ask for permission to list him or her as a reference. Be sure to double and triple check all phone numbers, cell phone numbers, and e-mail contact information for accuracy.

   You can include a list of your references with each resume you give out, or you can simply state at the end of the resume that you have references available. If you are responding to an advertisement, read it carefully to see whether you are supposed to send references. If the ad does not mention them, you probably do not need to send them with your resume. List your references on a separate sheet of paper, and remember to include your name, address, and phone number at the top of the list. For each reference that you list, provide the person's name, address, telephone number, and job title.

5. **Organizations.** It is a good idea to list any professional organizations related to the culinary arts that you belong to, for example, the International Association of Culinary Professionals (IACP) or the James Beard Foundation.

6. **Qualifications/certifications.** If you have earned any special certifications, such as the Certified Chef de Cuisine (CCC) offered by the American Culinary Federation or the ProChef Certification from the Culinary Institute of America, definitely list them prominently on your resume.

7. **Technology.** In many cases, you will be e-mailing your resume and cover letter to your prospective employers. If you attach your resume to an e-mail, be sure the filename on the attached document is your name (for example, *JohnSmithResume*), and not just *resume*. The employer will likely download many resumes and you want yours to be easily distinguished from the others. It is also a good idea to include the resume and cover letter in one document: If your cover letter is an e-mail and your resume is attached, the employer has to refer both to your e-mail and to the attachment. If you are applying by e-mail, make it easy for the employer to keep all your information in one document.

You may also want to consider using technology to showcase your talents even more. For example, post photographs of some of your best dishes to a website and embed a link to the site in the body of your cover letter. You could also start a blog about cooking to get exposure for your name. If well done, a blog could help you gain entry into the culinary world, opening up networking opportunities with others in the field. If you are comfortable asking colleagues or clients you have worked with to offer a quote or two about you, include those on your website or blog. In today's world, with its overwhelming amount of media, the little extras can really make a difference in getting an interview.

## How to Organize Your Resume

There are many ways of organizing a resume, but the three most common are

1. the chronological format,
2. the functional (or skills) format, and
3. the combination format.

In the first format you list the dates of your past employment in chronological order. This is a good format for people who have continuous work experience with little or no breaks in between jobs. The functional format, on the other hand, is more appropriate for people who have been absent from the workforce or who have large gaps in employment. In the functional format, you emphasize the skills or qualifications that you have rather than the dates of employment. The combination format fuses aspects of both the chronological and functional formats.

Choose the format that best highlights your training, experience, and expertise. Take a look at the sample resumes appearing on the next few pages to get ideas for creating your own resume. Other examples can be found online, or you can pick up a book on resumes from your local bookstore or library.

When you have finished writing your resume, ask someone you trust to read it and suggest ways to improve it.

## Sample Resumes

### Sample Chronological Resume

# Miguel T. Gomez, CC

242 West Palm Beach Ave.

Palm Beach, FL 33765

Phone: 123-456-7890

E-mail: mtgomez@gmail.com

## EXPERIENCE

2006–Present

Maria's Trattoria

West Palm Beach, Florida

*Line Cook*

Grill and sauté stations

Create dinner specials twice a week

Prepare soups and sauces daily

Volume restaurant, with 1,500+ covers per week

2001–2006

Celeste's Cafe

Ft. Lauderdale, Florida

*Prep Cook*

Prepared daily mise en place for various stations

Assisted cooks at pantry, grill, and sauté stations

## EDUCATION

Diploma in Culinary Arts from the Pinellas Technical Education Center, St. Petersburg, Florida, 2001.

Diploma. Countryside High School. Palm Harbor, Florida, 1999.

## QUALIFICATIONS AND SKILLS

- ▶ American Culinary Federation Certified Culinarian
- ▶ ServSafe Sanitation certified by National Restaurant Association
- ▶ Fluent in Spanish
- ▶ References provided upon request

**Philip Moore**

375 Elm St., Apt 3W

Anytown, USA 12345

Phone: 803-555-1487

Cell: 803-439-2957

E-mail: pmoore@internet.com

Objective: To gain an entry-level position as a line cook in a full-service restaurant preparing a wide range of international cuisines.

## KEY SKILLS

▶ Fast, precise and highly motivated worker

▶ Full mastery of basic cooking techniques with an emphasis on pastry skills

▶ Strong sense of teamwork and leadership and easily takes initiative

## EDUCATION

Classic Culinary School, 345 Main St., Lakeport, IL 12345, 675-555-3330

June 2008–December 2008

▶ Diploma in Culinary Arts, graduated with high honors

▶ Chef's Citation Award for excellence in International cuisine

Lakeport High School, 35 Park Blvd., Lakeport, IL 12345

September 2004–June 2008

▶ Diploma, graduated with honors, GPA 3.5

▶ President of student council

▶ Copresident of debate team

▶ Honors medal in English and History

## WORK EXPERIENCE

Franco's Italian Restaurant, 34 Elm St., Lakeport, IL 12345, chef/owner Mario Franco, 675-555-1234. November 2008–December 2008

Worked garde manger station for 6 weeks as part of culinary school externship program. Was given tasks including stocking, ingredient preparation, and simple plating of salads and appetizers. Prepared appetizers for corporate catered events during holiday season.

Jones Diner, 23 Oak St., Lakeport, IL 12345, owner Mark Douglas, 675-555-1283. January 2008–June 2008

Prepared salads and desserts in high-volume 50-seat diner setting featuring classic American food. Occasionally worked grill. Named employee of the month.

References available upon request.

The following resume focuses on the applicant's work experience.

## Christine Johnson

345 W. 103 St., Apt 3J

New York, NY 10025

212-456-1234

Cell phone: 555-893-7923

E-mail: cjohnson@internet.com

Objective: To work as a sous chef in a catering business setting

## WORK EXPERIENCE

Mediterranean Café, 425 Broadway, New York, NY 12345, chef/owner John Anderson, 212-456-3945. September 2008–Present

- ▶ Worked as line cook at James Beard–award winning 30-seat café/restaurant, $1 million rev annually, 3 line cooks
- ▶ Prepared average of 50 covers a night; specialties include fish and grilled meats as well as pasta station
- ▶ Created two new dishes that were added to regular menu
- ▶ Oversaw menu planning for all catered special events

Direct supervisor, Chef de Cuisine Mary Barnard

Custom Catering Service, 354 Broadway, New York, NY 10239, owner, Greg Marcus 212-567-3932. May 2008–September 2008

- ▶ Worked as a prep cook for corporate catering company servicing the media and fashion industry; specialty was light, health-conscious Italian food
- ▶ Oversaw on-site plating at events; supervised interns

## EDUCATION

Famous Culinary School, 345 E 27 St, New York, NY 12345, 212-444-5935. March 2007–May 2008

- ▶ Graduated with honors
- ▶ Worked as catering chef for corporate events
- ▶ Additional coursework in restaurant management

Cooper College, 3 Hill Ave., Cooper, PA 12956, 359-496-6790

Graduated with distinction in European history, Diploma June 2006

- ▶ Worked in college cafeteria kitchen as assistant during senior year

References available upon request.

**Sample Functional Resume**

# Madeleine LeTourneau, CSC

476 Sunnyside Drive

San Jose, CA 94302

415-784-2358

mlt@yahoo.com

Objective: Sous Chef or Chef de Cuisine

## QUALIFICATIONS

Two years of experience as a sous chef

American Culinary Federation Certified Sous Chef

Four years of experience as a line cook

Two years of training and supervising line cooks

Banquet and garde manger experience

## PROFESSIONAL EXPERIENCE

Prepared daily a variety of quality soups and sauces from scratch

Planned and cooked daily menu specials

Managed six line cooks, including hiring and firing as needed

Assisted executive chef in daily operation of kitchen

Skilled at containing food costs

Maintained ingredient inventory system

## EMPLOYMENT HISTORY

Sous Chef, A Touch of France, 2004–Present

Lead Cook and banquet work, Holiday Sun Resort, 1999–2004

Line Cook, Waterfront View, 1997–1999

Grill and Fry Cook, Tangy Tuesday's, 1996–1997

Pantry Cook, Sweetwater's, 1993–1996

Garde manger and banquet assistant, Hilton Resort, 1990–1993

## EDUCATION

A. O. S. Degree in Culinary Arts from the California Culinary Academy, San Francisco, 1996.

## AWARD

ACF Food Salon Silver Medal Winner, Junior Chef Competition, 1995.

**Sample Combination Resume**

# Lawrence Bing

320 Oak Grove Boulevard

Brooklyn, NY 10015

718-425-6842

**Objective:** Pastry Chef / Baker

## SUMMARY OF QUALIFICATIONS

One and a half years experience as pastry chef for prestigious country club

Mixed and baked cookies; formed and baked specialty breads for high-volume bakery

Baked, prepared, and decorated cakes and pastries using creative techniques

Prepared desserts for banquets and events for up to 500 guests

## PROFESSIONAL EXPERIENCE

Pastry Chef, River Heights Golf and Country Club

Long Island, NY, 2007–Present

Responsible for production of all baked goods for clubhouse banquets, including breads, desserts, and specialty items.

Baker, Larry's Bakeshop & Cafe

Brooklyn, NY, 2004–2007

Head baker of retail bakery; baked and decorated cookies, breads, pies, and cakes.

Pastry Chef Assistant, The Verazzano Hotel

Brooklyn, NY, 1999–2004

Assisted the pastry chef in all aspects of bakery production for the hotel's restaurant and room service. Helped bake and prepare specialty items for banquets.

## EDUCATION

A. A. S., Baking and Pastry Arts. Johnson & Wales University, Providence, RI, 1999

B. A., English. New York University, New York, NY, 1997

**Sample Career Changer Resume**

The following resume focuses on the applicant's skill set gained from years of work in another field.

# John Olsen

38 Babcock St., Apt 2R

Large City, MA 20495

Phone: 254-596-8940

Cell: 849-276-8379

E-mail: JohnO@hotmail.com

Objective: To use my skills in public speaking, organization, and specialty food knowledge as a culinary educator.

## KEY SKILLS

▶ Clear and effective communicator, strong interpersonal skills

▶ Experienced making presentations in front of groups of people

▶ Extensive knowledge of a range of cuisines, with a specialty in Southeast Asian cooking and ingredients

▶ Fluent in Spanish

## EDUCATION

Famous Culinary School, 345 E 27 St., New York, NY 12345, 212-444-5935. March 2008–July 2008

Completed culinary degree program on accelerated schedule, graduated with highest honors

Cooper College, 3 Hill Ave. Cooper, PA 12956, 359-496-6790.

Graduated with distinction in Spanish, Diploma June 2000

## TEACHING EXPERIENCE

Famous Culinary School, 345 E 27 St., New York, NY 12345, 212-444-5935. March 2008–July 2008

▶ Worked as teaching assistant in recreational classes while completing degree program.

Great Foods, 345 Second Avenue, New York, NY 10395, 212-394-6894. June 2008–July 2008

▶ Developed a program in conjunction with local supermarket to teach basic nutrition and cooking to children.

Personal Chef, New York

▶ Taught classes basic cooking techniques to individuals and groups in clients' homes

## PREVIOUS WORK HISTORY

Marketing and Sales Experience

Jones Marketing Company, New York, NY, 2004–2008

Sales representative

▶ Made group presentations and communicated product knowledge to customers

▶ Created and delivered marketing PowerPoint presentations for new client acquisition

Famous Retail Store, New York, NY, 2000–2004

Customer Service Manager

▶ Fielded customers' questions and resolved issues

References available upon request.

## COVER LETTER BASICS

Once your resume is looking perfect, it is time to concentrate on your cover letter. A cover letter is a way to introduce yourself to prospective employers. It should be brief and capture the employer's attention, and it should not repeat too much of what is in the resume. Also, cover letters should focus on highlighting your *skills*, not just provide a list of your past jobs. The goal of the cover letter is to interest the perspective employer even more in your background and experience. Be clear about the position you are applying for and proceed to discuss your particular skills that make you the best candidate for the job. Finally, show enthusiasm for the job in your cover letter and express your desire for an interview in a clear, straightforward manner.

Cover letters should follow a business letter format, and include the following information:

▶ the name and address of the specific person to whom the letter is addressed

▶ the name of the job you are applying for

▶ the reason for your interest in the company or position

▶ your main qualifications for the position (in brief)

▶ where you learned about the job (Internet job board, school career office, or whatever)

▶ a request for an interview

▶ your phone number and address

Take the time to do some investigating, so you can address your cover letter to someone specific if possible. Call the company or visit their website to see if you can identify the hiring manager's or human resources representative's name. If it is the company's policy not to give out names, at least get the person's formal title and use that in place of a name.

## Sample Cover Letters

Miguel T. Gomez

242 West Palm Beach Avenue

Palm Beach, FL 33765

123-456-7890

October 10, 2010

Ms. Stephani Jones

Executive Chef

Café European

451 Beach Tree Lane

West Palm Beach, FL 33745

Dear Chef Jones:

It is with great interest that I read your advertisement on Monster.com for a Lead Line Cook.

As you can see from my enclosed resume, I have headed the grill and sauté stations at Maria's Trattoria for four years. While in this position, I have become certified as a culinarian by the American Culinary Federation. I am experienced in planning and cooking dinner specials on a regular basis, and have been greatly praised by the executive chef and our customers for the creativity of my plate presentations. I have volunteered to manage the other line cooks and have done so on four separate occasions with outstanding results. My culinary skills, creativity, and teamwork ability make me an excellent candidate for this position.

Should you agree that my qualifications are a good match for your needs, please call me at 123-456-7890. I look forward to meeting you. Thank you in advance for your time and consideration.

Sincerely,


Miguel T. Gomez

Resume Enclosed


## Here's another example:

April 27, 2010

Jorge Smith

38 Brie St., Apt 2R

Cityfield, MA 20495

Phone: 254-596-8940

Cell: 849-276-8379

E-mail: jorgesmith435@internet.com


Mr. Rodney Jones

Great Cheese Company

1000 Fondue Road

Gouda, MA 01010

Dear Mr. Jones,

Thank you for considering my application for the position of retail cheese manager in your store. My experience includes not only solid background in identifying hundreds of international cheeses, but extensive experience serving customers as well.

Through my experience working at Great Foods supermarket, I was exposed not only to a great variety of international cheeses, but to classic as well contemporary cheesemaking techniques. I was responsible for ordering the majority of the cheeses as well as mer-chandising the department. Through study and additional research, I was able to bring into the store some little-known cheeses that proved to be successful sellers.

My customer service skills are also strong. Twice I earned an Employee of the Month award for assisting customers. I reorganized the department, which made it more ac-cessible to customers and resulted in an 8% increase in sales.

I would very much like to bring my experience and interest in artisanal cheese to your store. I believe I can use my background to help you grow your sales. I look forward to discussing this position further with you and to sharing my training and experience, out-lined in my attached resume.

Many thanks.

With best regards,

Jorge Smith

## THE INTERVIEW

You have sent your resume and cover letter; gotten the call to come in for the interview, and, now you are excited. What can you expect?

If you are applying for any job requiring hands-on work with food, pack your knives (make sure they are good and sharp!) and apron, and be ready to show your kitchen smarts if you are asked to do so.

In the interview, remember to emphasize not only your food savvy but also your teamwork, leadership, flexibility, curiosity, and stamina. And most of all, express your passion, the reason you are a culinary professional!

During the course of your culinary career, you will probably go on several job interviews. So it makes sense to spend some time going over interview basics, such as what to wear, how to answer and ask questions, and essentially how to make a great impression.

## Personal Appearance

While there is some flexibility in the dress code for culinary arts professionals who are job hunting, it is safe to assume that you should present yourself professionally for every interview. Exactly how you dress will depend on the type and level of the job you are seeking. For instance, experienced chefs may go on an interview dressed in their kitchen uniform, commonly known as their *whites*. However, a line cook may dress neatly in casual but clean and ironed pants and shirt. While you usually will not need to wear a corporate suit to an interview, you should strive to project a professional appearance.

### INTERVIEW TIPS

▶ Show enthusiasm and genuine interest in the position.

▶ Arrive early or exactly on time—before the day of the interview, visit your destination so you will know where to go.

▶ If you are asked about a skill you do not possess, admit it, but say you are willing to learn.

▶ Use standard formal English and avoid slang.

▶ Thank the interviewer at the completion of the interview.

## What to Do During the Interview

One of the most important things you can do during an interview is to relax and just *be yourself*. Often, an executive chef or other manager will say they hired someone just because they felt a connection with that person. Perhaps it was a gut feeling, or just a sense that this person would fit into their team. If you act stiff and uptight, the interviewer may not be able to see the real you and will not get that inner sense that you are the best person for the job.

Greet your interviewer with a firm handshake and make eye contact during the greeting. This is no time to be shy or timid. Focus on speaking confidently throughout the interview and answer questions in complete sentences, not just *yes* or *no*. On the other hand, do not ramble on too long answering any one question. A good rule of thumb is to keep your answers under two to three minutes each. Prepare carefully for each interview.

Learn as much as you can about the restaurant or establishment before the interview so you will sound knowledgeable when answering and asking questions during the interview.

### Answering Questions

It is a good idea to practice asking and answering sample interview questions with a friend or relative to brush up on your presentation and communication skills. Here are some of the most common interview questions along with tips on how to answer them.

*Tell me about yourself.*

Begin your answer with a short prepared statement that focuses on your training, qualifications, or work experience. You do not need to provide any personal information in your answer about your marital status, religion, age, or hobbies. For example:

> *I am a hard-working cook dedicated to professional growth and excellence, with four years of experience on the line, working the pantry, pasta, and grill stations. I have been told that I exhibit leadership skills, professionalism and respect for my colleagues.*

*What are your strengths and weaknesses?*

You can launch directly into your best strength and discuss it at length. Then briefly describe a weakness, followed by a strength. This way you sandwich a negative in between two positives. Whatever you do, do not spend more time talking about your weaknesses than you do about your strengths.

It may help to list your strengths and weaknesses on a piece of paper. After looking them over, select the top two strengths and the least damaging weakness and practice discussing them in preparation for this question. Be truthful, and do not use canned answers. For example, *My weakness is that I'm a perfectionist*, and *I'm a workaholic* are trite, overused, and may irritate your interviewer. But do figure out which of your weaknesses sounds least likely to cause a prospective employer concern and go with that one.

*What do you know about our restaurant[hotel/institution/food service operation]?*
This is the opportunity to impress the hiring manager by showing that you had the initiative and drive to research the company before you came to the interview. Perhaps you saw the restaurant's executive chef at a recent culinary competition and were impressed by her work. Or you read an article online praising the restaurant for using green practices. Make sure you have something positive to say.

*Why did you leave your last job?*
No matter how bad the circumstances may have been, always frame your reason in a positive light. You might want to say something like *I wanted more responsibility* or *I wanted to advance my career*. Never say it was because you hated your boss or could not get along with your colleagues.

*How many days were you absent from work in your last job?*
Of course you need to answer honestly, but be sure to phrase your answer in a positive light or offer an explanation for why you may have missed several days. If you did not miss any days, do not just say *zero* or *none*. Use the question as an opportunity to stress your high work ethic, sense of professionalism, or passion for excellence. For example, you might say, *I am proud to say that I did not miss one single day in my last position as line cook because I take my work very seriously, and I am committed to providing excellent service to the customers and to my employer.*

While you need to answer questions in an interview clearly and concisely, you also need to ask questions. Asking the right questions can help you to determine whether you really want to work for a particular organization.

## Asking Questions

At some point during the interview, the interviewer will most likely ask you if you have any questions. If she does not, you should bring it up yourself. You can simply say something like *I also have a few questions for you to help me get a better sense of the position*, and then plunge in. Have a list of questions ready to help you determine whether the position is a good fit for you. Remember, this is not a one-way street—you are also evaluating them. Besides, if you ask no questions, you may give the impression that you are not interested in the position.

Here are some sample interview questions. You may have some other questions, but you can use this list as a starting point.

▶ What would my typical day consist of?

▶ What would my level of responsibility be?

▶ What would my work hours be?

▶ How many customers do you serve daily or weekly?

▶ How long has this establishment been in business?

▶ How often do you change your menu?

▶ How many cooks work in this kitchen?

▶ What is the possibility for promotion?

▶ Do you team up trainees with experienced cooks? For how long?

▶ What type of benefits do you offer?

▶ What kind of incentives or bonuses are available?

Asking the right questions in an interview can give you the feedback you need to make a sound decision once your job offers start rolling in. While some interviews will inevitably go smoother than others, each one offers you a chance to practice and improve your interviewing skills. After each interview, remember to send a thank you note to follow up on the meeting.

## Following Up after the Interview

After the interview, send an e-mail or a handwritten note to thank the interviewer for the opportunity to speak with her or him. Mention the time and date of the original interview, briefly highlight your qualifications, and reiterate your interest in the job. The interviewer may need to see other applicants before making an offer, so do not get discouraged if you do not get a definite answer right away. Generally, a decision is reached within a few weeks. If you do not hear from an employer within the amount of time suggested during the interview, follow up with a telephone call or e-mail.

## The Informational Interview

In addition to participating in actual job interviews, you can also get helpful job-related information by going on informational interviews. An informational interview is different from a job interview because you are merely seeking information and not an actual job. It is a good way to familiarize yourself with a new culinary position or area of specialization. For example, if you have only worked in restaurants, and you are interested in landing a job in a corporate dining room or a hospital foodservice operation, you can contact someone who works in these areas and arrange an informational interview with them. Or, if you have never set foot into a professional kitchen but are interested in exploring it, you can start by asking several cooks a few questions. In order to make maximum use of the time a person is willing to spend with you, ask pertinent questions and be concise. Here is a list of questions that you can ask during an informational interview.

- What is your typical workday like?
- What things do you find most rewarding about your work?
- What are the toughest problems you encounter in your job?
- Please give me a general description of the work you do.
- What are the frustrations in your work?
- What educational degrees, professional certifications, or other credentials are needed for entry and advancement in this area?
- Do you belong to any professional associations? Do they provide job hunting assistance or post job openings?
- What abilities, interests, values, and personality characteristics are important for effectiveness and satisfaction in your field?
- How do people usually learn about job openings in your field?
- What types of employers, other than your own, hire people to perform the type of work you do?
- Do you know of any companies that offer entry-level training programs?
- If you were hiring someone for an entry-level position in your field, what would be the critical factors influencing your choice of one candidate over another?
- Is there anything else you think I would benefit from knowing about this field?

Conducting informational interviews will make you more knowledgeable about a particular job or area of specialization, and will also give you interview experience, which may lessen your anxiety in an actual job interview. Furthermore, informational interviews are an excellent opportunity for gaining networking contacts to help in your job search.

## EVALUATING YOUR JOB OFFERS

So you have been offered a job, or better yet, several jobs. Your task now is to evaluate each job opportunity. How does each job stack up against the others? Perhaps one will give you the chance to work with a highly respected chef, perhaps another is right next door to your home, perhaps a third comes with an excellent benefits package. For many jobs, the places that offer you a position will not expect you to accept or reject an offer on the spot. You will probably have a week or more to make up your mind. You need to consider all your options, review your notes from each interview, and then make a list of the pros and cons for accepting each job. The last step is to review your lists and choose the company that is the right fit for you. Once you have landed the job, you can focus on how to succeed in your new job.

*Some people like to paint pictures, or do gardening or build a boat in the basement. Other people get a tremendous pleasure out of the kitchen, because cooking is just as creative and imaginative an activity as drawing, woodcarving, or music.*

—Julia Child

# Appendix A

## Illustrations

## The Food Pyramid

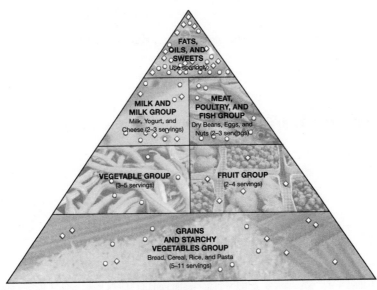

Adapted from USDA and USDHHS.

## Chef's Knives

From left: French knives (first three in row), boning knife, granton-style edge French knife, paring knife, tourné knife.

## How to Sharpen a Knife

1. Start with the knife nearly vertical, with the blade resting on the steel's inner side. 2. Rotate the wrist holding the knife as the blade moves along the steel in a downward motion. 3. Keep the blade in contact with the steel until the tip is drawn off the steel. Repeat the process with the blade resting on the steel's outer side.

## Pans in the Kitchen for Stovetop Cooking

Clockwise from bottom left: sauteuse (two nested), two saucepans (with lids), stockpot (with lid), sautoir (with lid).

## Common Kitchen Tools

Clockwise from left: balloon whip, sauce whip, fish spatula, kitchen fork, wide perforated offset spatula, French rolling pin, ball bearing rolling pin, swivel-bladed peelers, offset palette knives.

## Basic Knife Cuts

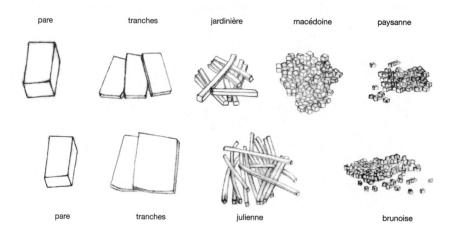

pare          tranches          jardinière          macédoine          paysanne

pare          tranches          julienne          brunoise

## Lamb Cuts

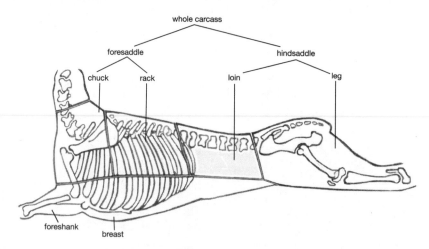

# Beef Cuts

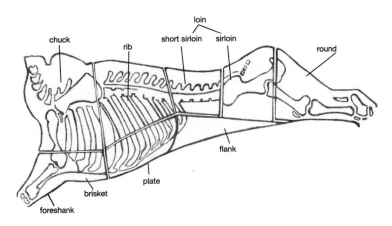

# Pork Cuts

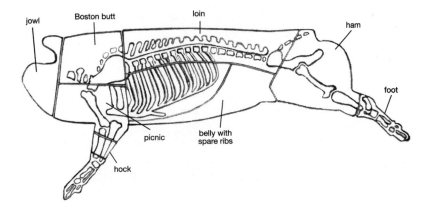

## Veal Cuts

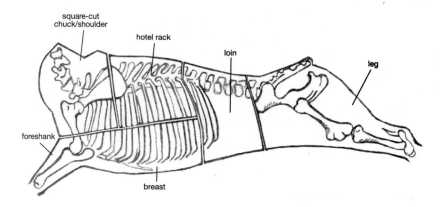

- square-cut chuck/shoulder
- hotel rack
- loin
- leg
- foreshank
- breast

## Poultry Cuts

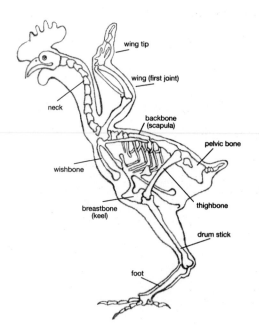

- wing tip
- wing (first joint)
- neck
- backbone (scapula)
- pelvic bone
- wishbone
- thighbone
- breastbone (keel)
- drum stick
- foot

## Flat Fish Cuts

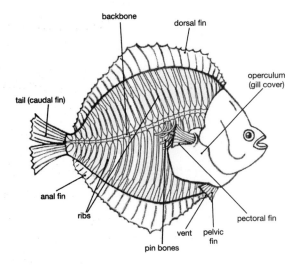

## Round Fish Cuts

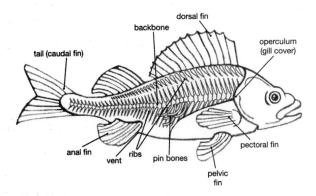

# Appendix B

## Job Resources

**THE FOLLOWING** is a list of online resources to help you land your culinary job. When using the various databases, search using such terms as *cook*, *cooking*, *culinary*, *food*, *foodservice worker*, *hospitality*, *restaurant*, *chef*, *baker*, and other food-related terms to find specific jobs geared toward your skills.

Many of the websites will also allow you to post your resume (to help employers find you) as well as sign up for e-mail alerts and RSS feeds by which you receive updates on available jobs on a regular basis. Some also provide articles on culinary related topics, industry information, career advice, educational opportunities, seminars, and networking opportunities.

If you are currently a culinary student, or have recently graduated, be sure to check out your school's placement office. Many schools have their own database of jobs that are not listed for the public on the Internet.

Career Builder

www.careerbuilder.com/

Craig's List (search under food/bev/hosp)

www.craigslist.org/about/sites

Hound

www.hound.com

Indeed

www.indeed.com/q-Cook-jobs.html

Jobs.com

www.jobs.com/

Monster

www.monster.com/

The National Restaurant Association job bank

www.restaurant.org/careers/

Snag A Job

www.snagajob.com/

Simply Hired

www.simplyhired.com/a/jobs/list/q-cooking

StarChefsJobfinder.com

www.starchefsjobfinder.com/

Yahoo!

http://hotjobs.yahoo.com/

*When we no longer have good cooking in the world, we will have no literature, no high and sharp intelligence, nor friendly gatherings, nor social harmony.*

—Marie-Antoine Carême

# Appendix C

## Culinary Schools

**THE AMERICAN** Culinary Federation Foundation Accrediting Commission currently accredits over 165 culinary training programs in the United States. Completion of these programs can lead to earning an associate's degree, certificate, or diploma in the culinary arts.

The following is a sampling of some of the best-known culinary arts schools and programs in the United States. To find a school in your area not included in this list, consult the online resources list at the end of this Appendix.

**Culinary Institute of America—Hyde Park**
**Admissions Department**
**1946 Campus Dr., Hyde Park, NY 12538**
**800-CULINARY (800-285-4627) or**
   **845-452-9430**
**admissions@culinary.edu**
**www.cia.edu**

California Branch
The Culinary Institute of America at
   Greystone
2555 Main St.
St. Helena, CA 94574
800-CULINARY (800-285-4627) or
   800-888-7850

Becoming a **CULINARY ARTS PROFESSIONAL**

Texas Branch

The Culinary Institute of America, San
   Antonio

312 Pearl Pkwy., Bdg. 3

San Antonio, TX 78215

800-CULINARY (800-285-4627) or
   210-222-1113

ciasanantonio@culinary.edu

French Culinary Institute—New York

462 Broadway

New York, NY 10013

888-FCI-CHEF (888-324-2433)

www.frenchculinary.com

Florida Culinary Institute

2410 Metrocentre Blvd.

West Palm Beach, FL 33407

561-842-8324

www.floridaculinaryinstitute.net/

Institute of Culinary Education

Career Training Division

50 W. 23 St. # 5

New York, NY 10010

212-847-0700

888-354-CHEF (888-354-2433)

www.iceculinary.com

International Culinary Schools at the Art
   Institutes

offer culinary programs at 30 Art Institutes
   schools

www.artinstitutes.edu/culinary-arts.aspx

Johnson & Wales University

8 Abbott Park Pl.

Providence, RI 02903

800-DIAL-JWU (800-342-5598)

http://www.jwu.edu/

Keiser University Center for Culinary Arts

Melbourne Campus

900 S. Babcock St.

Melbourne, FL 32901

321-255-2255

   Sarasota Campus

   866-Keiser2 (866-534-7372)

   Tallahassee Campus

   877-CHEF123 (877-243-3123)

   www.keiseruniversity.edu/culinary/
      school_melb2.html

L'Academie de Cuisine

Professional Culinary Training

16006 Industrial Dr.

Gaithersburg, MD 20877

301-670-8670 or 800-664-CHEF
   (800-664-2433)

info@lacademie.com

www.lacademie.com/

Le Cordon Bleu College of Culinary Arts

Various locations around the country

   Le Cordon Bleu College of Culinary
      Arts in Atlanta

   1927 Lakeside Pkwy.

   Tucker, GA 30084

   888-549-8222

   www.chefs.edu/

Texas Culinary Academy
11400 Burnet Rd., Ste. 2100
Austin, TX 78758
888-559-7222

Le Cordon Bleu College of Culinary
  Arts in Boston
215 First St.
Cambridge, MA 02142
888-394-6222

The Cooking and Hospitality Institute of
  Chicago
361 West Chestnut
Chicago, IL 60610
888-295-7222

Le Cordon Bleu Institute of Culinary
  Arts in Dallas
11830 Webb Chapel Rd. #1200
Dallas, TX 75234
888-495-5222

Le Cordon Bleu College of Culinary
  Arts in Las Vegas
1451 Center Crossing Rd.
Las Vegas, NV 89144
888-551-8222

Le Cordon Bleu College of Culinary
  Arts in Los Angeles
Pasadena Location
521 E. Green St.
Pasadena, CA 91101
866-230-9450

Hollywood Location
6370 W. Sunset Blvd.
Hollywood, CA 90028
866-230-9450

Le Cordon Bleu College of Culinary
  Arts in Miami
3221 Enterprise Way
Miramar, FL 33025
888-569-3222

Le Cordon Bleu College of Culinary
  Arts in Minneapolis/St.Paul
1315 Mendota Heights Rd.
Mendota Heights, MN 55120
888-348-5222

Le Cordon Bleu College of Culinary
  Arts in Orlando
8511 Commodity Cir., Ste. 100
Orlando, FL 32819
888-793-3222

Pennsylvania Culinary Institute
717 Liberty Avenue
Pittsburgh, PA 15222
888-314-8222

Le Cordon Bleu College of Culinary
  Arts in Portland
600 S.W. 10 Ave., Ste. 400
Portland, OR 97205
888-891-6222

Le Cordon Bleu College of Culinary
  Arts in Sacramento
2450 Del Paso Rd.
Sacramento, CA 95834
888-807-8222

California Culinary Academy
350 Rhode Island St.
San Francisco, CA 94103
888-897-3222

Le Cordon Bleu College of Culinary
Arts in Scottsdale
8100 East Camelback Rd., Ste. 1001
Scottsdale, AZ 85251
888-557-4222

Le Cordon Bleu College of Culinary
Arts in Seattle
360 Corporate Dr. North
Tukwila, WA 98188
888-909-7222

Le Cordon Bleu College of Culinary
Arts in St. Louis
7898 Veterans Memorial Pkwy.
St Peters, MO 63376
866-951-7222

Bachelor of Arts in Le Cordon Bleu
Culinary Management Online
888-557-4222

The Professional Culinary Institute of
California
700 W. Hamilton Ave.
Campbell, CA 95008
1-866-318-CHEF (866-318-2433)
admissions@pcichef.com
www.professionalculinaryinstitute.com/
index.shtml

San Diego Culinary Institute
Admissions Office
8024 La Mesa Blvd.
La Mesa, CA 91941
619-644-2100
info@sdci-inc.com
www.sdci-inc.com/contact.html

Careers Through Culinary Arts (a training
program for high school students)
250 W. 57 St., Ste. 2015
New York, NY 10107
212-974-7111 (fax: 212-974-7117)
www.ccapinc.org

The Natural Gourmet
48 W. 21 St., 2nd Fl.
New York, NY 10010
212-645-5170
naturalgourmetinstitute.com

Many community colleges offer very reputable culinary arts programs. Check with your local school for more details.

**To find additional schools not listed here, try the following online resources.**

The National Restaurant Association (NRA) offers a state-by-state guide to culinary and hospitality schools, as well as other food related programs at www.restaurant.org/careers/schools.cfm.

The NRA also includes a career-building program for high school students interested in the culinary arts. See http://prostart.restaurant.org/ for more information.

The StarChefs website offers a school finder at www.starchefs.com/cooking_school_finder/html/.

The Chef 2Chef website offers a list of culinary schools at www.chef2chef.net/rank/schools.html.

AllCulinarySchools offers a searchable database of culinary schools at www.allculinaryschools.com/contact/index.php.

Culinary School Guide offers access to over 165 accredited culinary programs at http://affiliate.collegesurfing.com/culinary-school-guide/.

The Cooking Schools website offers a searchable database of culinary schools by state and city and information on various programs and degrees, as well as articles on cooking, at www.cookingschools.com.

# Appendix D

## Culinary Certification

**AS DISCUSSED** in Chapter 3, there are several national organizations that offer culinary certifications, including the Culinary Institute of America, the National Restaurant Association, the American Culinary Federation, and the National Registry.

The following is a list of certifications currently offered by the American Culinary Federation. The ACF has fourteen levels of professional certifications for cooks and chefs ranging from entry-level to master chef. Earning these types of certifications as you progress throughout your career can help you continually increase your skills and knowledge, set you apart from other candidates, and help you to land jobs.

## COOKING PROFESSIONALS

*Certified Culinarian® (CC®):* An entry-level culinarian within a commercial foodservice operation responsible for preparing and cooking sauces, cold food, fish, soups and stocks, meats, vegetables, eggs, and other food items.

*Certified Sous Chef™ (CSC™):* A chef who supervises a shift or station(s) in a foodservice operation. Equivalent job titles are sous chef, banquet chef, garde manger, first cook, A.M. sous chef, and P.M. sous chef.

*Certified Chef de Cuisine® (CCC®):* A chef who is the supervisor in charge of food production in a foodservice operation, whether a single unit of a multiunit operation or a free-standing operation. He or she is in essence the chef of the operation with the final decision-making power as it relates to culinary operations.

*Certified Executive Chef® (CEC®):* A chef who is the department head usually responsible for all culinary units in a restaurant, hotel, club, hospital, or foodservice establishment, or the owner of a foodservice operation. In addition to culinary responsibilities, other duties include budget preparation, payroll, maintenance, controlling food costs, and maintaining financial and inventory records.

*Certified Master Chef® (CMC®):* The consummate chef. A CMC® possesses the highest degree of professional culinary knowledge, skill, and mastery of cooking techniques. A separate application is required, in addition to successfully completing an eight-day testing process judged by peers. Certification as a CEC® or CEPC® is a prerequisite.

## PERSONAL COOKING PROFESSIONALS

*Personal Certified Chef™ (PCC™):* A chef who is engaged in the preparation, cooking, and serving of foods on a cook-for-hire basis. Must also have knowledge of menu planning, marketing, financial management, and operational decision making. Has at least three years of cooking experience and one full year of Personal Chef experience.

*Personal Certified Executive Chef™ (PCEC™):* An advanced chef who is engaged in the preparation, cooking, and serving of foods on a cook-for-hire basis. Must also have knowledge of menu planning, marketing, financial management, and operational decision making. Has at least three years of Personal Chef experience.

## BAKING AND PASTRY PROFESSIONALS

*Certified Pastry Culinarian® (CPC®):* An entry-level culinarian within a pastry foodservice operation responsible for the preparation and production of pies, cookies, cakes, breads, rolls, desserts, or other baked goods.

*Certified Working Pastry Chef® (CWPC®):* A pastry chef who supervises a pastry section or a shift within a foodservice operation and has considerable responsibility for preparation and production of all pastry items.

*Certified Executive Pastry Chef® (CEPC®):* A pastry chef who is a department head, usually responsible to the executive chef of a food operation or to the management of a pastry specialty firm. A CEPC® has supervisory responsibility as well as administrative duties.

*Certified Master Pastry Chef® (CMPC®):* A CMPC® possesses the highest degree of professional knowledge, skill, and mastery of cooking techniques as they apply to baking and pastry. A separate application is required, in addition to successfully completing an eight-day testing process judged by peers. Certification as a CEC® or CEPC® is a prerequisite.

## CULINARY ADMINISTRATORS

*Certified Culinary Administrator™ (CCA™):* This is an executive-level chef who is responsible for the administrative functions of running a professional foodservice operation. This culinary professional must demonstrate proficiency in culinary knowledge, human resources, operational management, and business planning skills.

## CULINARY EDUCATORS

*Certified Secondary Culinary Educator® (CSCE®):* An advanced-degree culinary professional who is working as an educator at an accredited secondary or vocational institution. A CSCE® is responsible for the development, implementation, administration, evaluation, and maintenance of a culinary arts or foodservice management curriculum. In addition, a CSCE® demonstrates the culinary competencies of a CCC® or CWPC® during a Practical Exam.

*Certified Culinary Educator™ (CCE™):* An advanced-degree culinary professional, with industry experience, who is working as an educator in an accredited postsecondary institution or military training facility. A CCE™ is responsible for the development, implementation, administration, evaluation, and maintenance of a culinary arts or foodservice management curriculum. In addition, a CCE™ demonstrates the culinary competencies of a CCC® or CWPC® during a Practical Exam.

*Source:* www.acfchefs.org.

# Appendix E

## Practice Test Answers

## PRACTICE TEST 1

### Skill Set 1: Basic Culinary Concepts and Methods

**Baking Skills**

1. b
2. c
3. False
4. a
5. True
6. d
7. c
8. a
9. b
10. d

### Braising Skills

11. b
12. a
13. a
14. c
15. d
16. b
17. b
18. c
19. c
20. d

### Grilling Skills

21. a
22. d
23. True
24. d
25. a
26. True
27. b
28. c
29. b
30. b

### Pastry Skills

31. a
32. d
33. d
34. True
35. d
36. d
37. c
38. b
39. b

## Poaching Skills

40. b
41. a
42. b
43. a
44. d
45. a

## Roasting Skills

46. a
47. b
48. True
49. c
50. False
51. a
52. c

## Sauce-Making Skills

53. d
54. b
55. a
56. a
57. a
58. a
59. a
60. c
61. b
62. d
63. b
64. a
65. d

### Stewing Skills

66. a
67. b
68. b
69. a

### Stock-Making Skills

70. a
71. c
72. a
73. a
74. b
75. d
76. a
77. a
78. d
79. a

## Skill Set 2: Core Competencies

### Knife Skills

80. c
81. b
82. a
83. d
84. a
85. b
86. a
87. a
88. b
89. c

**Weights and Measures Skills**

90. c
91. b
92. a
93. a
94. a
95. c
96. True
97. c

**Culinary Math Skills**

98. d
99. c
100. b
101. a

# Skill Set 3: Food Safety and Proper Food Handling

102. d
103. a
104. d
105. b
106. True
107. True
108. a
109. False
110. a
111. True

## Skill Set 4: Principles of Plating

112. c
113. d
114. d
115. d
116. c
117. b
118. d
119. a
120. b
121. b

## Skill Set 5: Organization of a Professional Kitchen

122. a
123. b
124. c
125. c
126. b
127. c
128. a
129. d
130. d
131. a
132. a

## PRACTICE TEST 2

## Skill Set 1: Basic Culinary Concepts and Methods

### Baking Skills

1. c
2. a
3. a
4. True
5. d
6. c
7. True
8. b
9. a
10. a

### Braising Skills

11. d
12. b
13. a
14. d
15. b
16. True
17. False
18. True
19. False
20. True
21. False

### Grilling Skills

22. b
23. a
24. False
25. a

26. d
27. True
28. c
29. b
30. c
31. d

## Pastry Skills

32. True
33. a
34. c
35. d
36. a
37. b
38. a
39. a
40. c
41. d

## Poaching Skills

42. d
43. b
44. a
45. d

## Roasting Skills

46. b
47. b
48. c
49. a

## Sauce-Making Skills

50. c
51. d
52. d
53. b
54. a
55. c
56. a
57. a
58. a
59. c

## Sauté Skills

60. b
61. b
62. True
63. b
64. a
65. b
66. c
67. True
68. d

## Stewing Skills

69. b
70. True
71. a

## Stock-Making Skills

72. a
73. a
74. c
75. d
76. b

77.  a
78.  a
79.  b
80.  a
81.  b

## Skill Set 2: Core Competencies

### Knife Skills

82.  b
83.  a
84.  a
85.  d
86.  d
87.  b
88.  a
89.  c
90.  a
91.  d
92.  b

### Weights and Measures Skills

93. True
94. c
95. d
96. b
97. False
98. a
99. d
100. a
101. b

**Culinary Math Skills**

102. d
103. c
104. c
105. b
106. c

## Skill Set 3: Food Safety and Proper Food Handling

107. d
108. b
109. a
110. a
111. a
112. a
113. True
114. c
115. b
116. a

## Skill Set 4: Principles of Plating

117. c
118. c
119. a
120. c
121. a
122. a

## Skill Set 5: Organization of a Professional Kitchen

123. a
124. a
125. b
126. b
127. b
128. b
129. c
130. c
131. b
132. c

# Glossary of Essential Culinary Terms

**A**

**acids.** Foods that have a sharp or tart flavor, which occurs naturally in vinegars, citrus juices, some wines, and fermented milk products. Acids can act as tenderizers.

**aioli.** A garlic mayonnaise popular as a condiment.

**a la carte.** A menu from which those dining make individual selections and each item is priced separately, as opposed to *prix fixe* where all courses are provided for a complete meal at a set price.

**al dente.** Cooked, but still firm rather than soft.

**allumette** (also called julienne). A vegetable cut into the size of matchsticks.

**aromatics.** Flavor and fragrance enhancers, such as herbs, spices, vinegars, wines, and even citrus and other fruits.

**arrowroot.** A thickener that remains clear when cooked.

**as-purchased (AP) weight.** The amount of the item before trimming or preparation, as opposed to the *EP* weight, which is the edible portion.

**B**

**bacteria.** Microscopic organisms that can either be beneficial or contaminate food.

**bain-marie.** Hot water used to cook food gently by surrounding a cooking pot with simmering water. It is also refers to steam table inserts or other devices that warm a finished product.

**baking powder.** A chemical that contains both acid and alkaline ingredients and leavens doughs and batters.

**baking soda.** Sodium bicarbonate. When combined with an acidic ingredient, it causes dough to rise.

**barbecue.** To grill over a wood or charcoal fire, brushing a marinade or sauce over the food in the process.

**bard.** To baste a lean meat during roasting using strips of fat.

**baste.** To prevent food from drying out while cooking by moistening with its own or other liquids.

**baton** or **batonnet.** A vegetable cut into sizes somewhat larger than allumette.

**binder.** An ingredient used to hold other ingredients together or to thicken a sauce.

**blanching.** To immerse food briefly in boiling water or fat.

**boiling.** To cook food in a liquid that has reached its highest possible temperature of 212°F.

**botulism.** A food-borne illness caused by bacteria.

**bouillon.** The French word for broth.

**bouquet garni.** A bundle of herbs tied together used as flavoring.

**braise.** To sear in fat, then simmer, covered, at a low temperature in a small amount of liquid.

**brigade system.** A system of kitchen organization in which each position has a station and specific responsibilities.

**brine.** Salt, water, and seasonings.

**broil.** To cook using a heat source above the food.

## C

**calorie.** A measure of food energy.

**caramelize.** To heat until melted and brown, for example sugar or onions.

**carbohydrate.** One of the basic nutrients the body uses for energy, including sugars, starches, and fibers.

**carry-over cooking.** Continuation of cooking even after removal from heat.

**charcuterie.** Cooking or working with cooked or processed pork and other meat items such as sausage, hams, pâtés, and terrines.

**chiffonade.** Shredded leafy vegetables or herbs used as a garnish.

**clarify.** To remove solid impurities from a liquid or from melted butter.

**confit.** Meat or poultry cooked and preserved in its own fat.

**convection oven.** An oven in which currents of hot forced air circulate around the food, cooking it evenly and rapidly.

**coulis.** The thickened juices of cooked foods.

**crème anglaise.** A custard made with milk, sugar, eggs, and vanilla.

**cross-contamination.** The transferring of a disease-causing element from one element to another by unwashed hands or on cutting boards, countertops, knives, and other kitchen tools.

**cure.** To preserve by salting, pickling, drying, or smoking.

### D

**danger zone.** The temperature from 40°F to 140°F that is most favorable for rapid growth of pathogens.

**deep fry.** To immerse food in hot fat to cook.

**deglaze.** To add liquid to a pan to loosen food particles, and then use the mixture that results to make a sauce.

**dice.** To cut into evenly sized small cubes.

**dredge.** To coat with a dry ingredient.

### E

**edible-portion (EP) weight.** The amount of the item after trimming or preparation, as opposed to the as-purchased (*AP*) weight.

**emincer.** To slice meat into very thin servings.

### F

**fat.** One of the basic nutrients the body uses for energy.

**fermentation.** The period of rising for yeast doughs and the breaking down of sugars in spirit-making.

**fiber.** Roughage, the nondigestible component of plants that is necessary to the human diet.

**FIFO.** First in first out: a basic principle of stock rotation whereby the oldest product is always used first.

**fillet.** A boneless cut of meat or fish.

**food-borne illness.** Sickness caused by eating adulterated or contaminated food. Usually two or more people must become ill after eating the same food before health officials make an official determination.

**free range.** Unconfined livestock.

**fructose.** Simple sugar found in fruits; the sweetest simple sugar.

# G

**garnish.** A decorative accompaniment to food.

**glaze.** To give food a shiny surface.

**grill.** To cook using a fire (gas, electric, charcoal, or wood) underneath the food.

# H

**HACCP.** (Hazard Analysis Critical Control Point). Food-tracking system that monitors food from receipt until it is served to customers. The goal is to make sure food is free from contamination. Includes time and temperature standards and safe handling practices.

**hors d'oeuvre.** An appetizer.

# I

**induction burner.** A heating unit that is faster than traditional burners because of magnetic attraction between the cooktop and metals in the pot.

**instant-read thermometer.** A thermometer that instantly measures the internal temperature of foods.

# J

**julienne.** To cut vegetables or other foods into flat strips measuring roughly $\frac{1}{8}$ inch $\times \frac{1}{8}$ inch $\times 2\frac{1}{2}$ inches.

**jus.** Juice, often used in the phrase *au jus*, meaning served in its own juice.

# K

**knead.** To mix dough by hand.

**kosher salt.** Salt that does not contain magnesium carbonate and therefore does not cloud solutions.

## L

**lactose.** The simple sugar in milk; it produces allergic reactions in a large number of individuals.

**leavening.** Baking powder, yeast, baking soda, or other substance that causes baked goods to rise.

**legume.** Bean or pea.

## M

**mandoline.** A stainless-steel slicing device.

**marinade.** A liquid or dry flavor added to foods before cooking.

**meringue.** Egg whites beaten with sugar until stiff.

**mince.** To chop into tiny pieces.

**minute, à la.** A restaurant production method where dishes are not prepared in advance but as the orders arrive in the kitchen.

**mise en place.** The assembling of all the ingredients, pans, utensils, and serving pieces needed for a particular dish.

**mollusk.** Clam, oyster, snail, octopus, or squid.

**MSG.** (Monosodium glutamate). A flavor enhancer that has no distinct flavor of its own. Derived from glutamic acid, it causes allergic reactions in some individuals.

**mousse.** A sweet or savory foam made from beaten egg whites and/or whipped cream and folded into a base.

## N

**nouvelle cuisine.** A culinary movement that emphasizes fresh, light, natural ingredients in innovate combinations, simply prepared and presented.

**nutrient.** The basic component of food—carbohydrates, fats, proteins, vitamins, and minerals—from which the body grows, repairs, and generates energy.

## O

**omega-3 fatty acids.** Polyunsaturated fatty acids that occur in fatty fish, dark green leafy vegetables, and some nuts and oils. They are believed to stimulate the immune system, reduce the risk of heart disease, lower blood pressure, and stunt the growth of tumors.

## P

**pan fry.** To cook in fat in a skillet, using more fat than sautéing but less than deep frying.

**parchment.** Heat-resistant cooking paper.

**pathogen.** A disease-causing element.

**perishable.** Refers to animal-based products (meat, poultry, fish, shellfish, and dairy products, cooked and uncooked), cooked vegetables, rice, pasta, potatoes, and other products that spoil easily.

**pilaf.** Grain sautéed briefly before it is simmered.

**poach.** To cook in hot liquid; typically reserved for such delicate foods as eggs and fish.

**poissonier.** The chef responsible for fish and their sauces.

**polyunsaturated fat.** Commonly found in corn, cottonseed, safflower, soy, and sunflower oils; the molecules have more than one bonding site.

**prix fixe.** A menu where all courses are provided for a complete meal at a set price. As opposed to *à la carte*, a menu from which those dining make individual selections and each item is priced separately.

**proof.** To allow a yeasted product to rise under controlled temperature and humidity.

**protein.** One of the basic nutrients, obtainable from animal and vegetable sources, that the body needs for energy, repair, and hormonal activity.

**puree.** To make into a smooth paste.

## Q

**quick bread.** A batter bread, made without kneading or fermentation, using chemical leaveners rather than yeast.

## R

**reduce.** To thicken by cooking out some of the liquid.

**rest.** To let food sit before carving to allow the juices to seep back in.

**remouillage.** A weak stock made from resimmered bones that have already been used to make stock.

**roux.** A mixture of equal parts fat and flour used to thicken sauces and soups.

## S

**sanitation.** The maintenance of a clean food-preparation environment by healthy food workers.

**saturated fat.** Found in coconut and palm oils, cocoa butter, meat, eggs, butter, and cheese; the bonding site is totally filled with hydrogen.

**saucier.** The chef responsible for sautéed items and their sauces.

**sauté.** To cook quickly in a small amount of fat in a flat pan on the stovetop.

**savory.** Not sweet.

**scald.** To heat a liquid to just below the boiling point.

**score.** To cut the surface at determined intervals for cooking or decorative purposes.

**sear.** To brown the surface over high heat.

**simmer.** To maintain the temperature just below boiling.

**smoke point.** The temperature at which fat begins to break.

**sodium.** An element necessary in small amounts for human nutrition; a component of cooking salts.

**stir-fry.** To sauté over very high heat, using little fat, and keeping the food moving constantly.

**stock.** A flavorful liquid made from simmering bones and/or vegetables in water.

**sweat.** To cook over low heat in a small amount of fat, in a covered pan or pot.

## T

**thermophilic.** Heat-loving; used to describe certain bacteria.

**toque.** A tall, pleated white hat worn by chefs.

**total utilization.** Using as much of a product as possible to prevent waste and maximize profits.

**tranche.** A slice, especially on the bias to enhance appearance.

## U

**unsaturated fat.** Of vegetable origin, and the bonding site is not filled with hydrogen.

## V

**vinaigrette.** A cold sauce, usually three parts oil to one part vinegar.

## W

**walk-in refrigerator.** A cooling unit large enough to maintain zones of temperature and humidity to store various foods properly.

## Y

**yeast.** A fungus that ferments.

## Z

**zest.** Thin, brightly colored outer rind of citrus, which contains flavorful oils.

# Additional Online Practice

**WHETHER YOU** need help building basic skills or preparing for an exam, visit the LearningExpress Practice Center! On this site, you can access additional practice materials. Using the code below, you'll be able to log and answer even more culinary arts practice questions. This online practice will also provide you with:

- ▶ **Immediate scoring**
- ▶ **Detailed answer explanations**
- ▶ **Personalized recommendations for further practice and study**

Log in to the LearningExpress Practice Center by using URL: **www.learnatest.com/practice**

This is your Access Code: **7397**

Follow the steps online to redeem your access code. After you've used your access code to register with the site, you will be prompted to create a username and password. For easy reference, record them here:

**Username:**_____    **Password:**_____

With your username and password, you can log in and answer these practice questions as many times as you like. If you have any questions or problems, please contact LearningExpress customer service at 1-800-295-9556 ext. 2, or e-mail us at **customerservice@learning expressllc.com.**

# NOTES

**NOTES**